TWO KAFKA PLAYS

TWO
KAFKA PLAYS

Kafka's Dick
and
The Insurance Man

ALAN BENNETT

faber and faber
LONDON · BOSTON

First published in 1987
by Faber and Faber Limited
3 Queen Square London WC1N 3AU
Reprinted 1988
Reprinted with amendments 1991

Typeset by Goodfellow & Egan, Cambridge
Printed in England by Clays Ltd, St Ives plc
All rights reserved

A CIP record for this book
is available from the British Library

ISBN 0-571-14727-5

Contents

Author's Note

I have written two plays around if not altogether about Kafka and in the process have accumulated a good deal of material about and around the Prague insurance man. Some of this is fanciful; sketches and speculations that never had a hope of being included in either piece; some of it is the kind of stuff that's always left over after writing a play, the speeches one has not managed to get in or the jokes that have had to be cut out and which are invariably the jokes and the speeches of which the playwright is most fond. Indeed he often thinks them the heart of the play, whereas the director (who never had to sweat over them) can see they're diversions, distractions or ornament. Not wanted on voyage. There is a word for this kind of thing which I have just come across (and having come across it can't think how I've managed so long without it); it is *paralipomena* – the things omitted but which appertain and are put in later as afterthoughts. It describes half my life as well as the notes that follow.

Besides these notes I have also included, as an introduction to *The Insurance Man*, a diary that I kept during the shooting of the film, which was first shown on BBC2 in February 1986. *Kafka's Dick* was produced at the Royal Court Theatre six months later. The play was not as well received by the critics as was the film and, though I could not imagine it better done and it played to packed houses, it did not transfer for a longer run. Shortly after it opened, I was working in Yugoslavia and drove into Italy for the day. Depressed about the reception the play had had I came by chance on the village of Aquileia, went to look at the church and found there a huge mosaic floor laid down in the fourth century. I say 'by chance' but to read Kafka is to become aware of coincidence. This is to put it at its mildest. His work prefigures the future, often in ways that are both specific and dreadful and this is part of his popular reputation. Sometimes though, his premonitions are less haunted, lighthearted even: he has a notion of the answering machine, for instance, and a dream of Berlin divided by a wall that seems more strange than tragic. In *Kafka's Dick*,

vii

Kafka is metamorphosed from a tortoise and is also sensitive about the size of his cock. So to find inside the west door of this church at Aquileia, a mosaic of a cock fighting a tortoise seemed not quite an accident. In the play cock and tortoise are not symbols; in Aquileia, so said the guide book, they represent a battle between the forces of light and darkness. I bought a postcard of the mosaic and the postcard-seller told me of a better example in the crypt. This took some finding, as the tortoise wasn't so much in the crypt as in a crypt beyond the crypt, and even there hidden behind the furthest pillar, just where Kafka (were he a tortoise) would have chosen to be. This seemed if not quite a nod then at least a wink and I drove on in better spirits.

I would like to thank Richard Eyre, who directed the play and the film (and who was always in good spirits) and for her unstinting help and encouragement, the best of editors, Mary Kay Wilmers.

ALAN BENNETT

Introduction

There are many perils in writing about Kafka. His work has been garrisoned by armies of critics with some 15,000 books about him at the last count. As there is a Fortress Freud so is there a Fortress Kafka, Kafka his own castle. For admission a certain high seriousness must be deemed essential and I am not sure I have it. One is nervous about presuming even to write his name, wanting to beg pardon for doing so, if only because Kafka was so reluctant to write his name himself. Like the Hebrew name of God it is a name that should not be spoken, particularly by an Englishman. In his dreams Kafka once met an Englishman. He was in a good grey flannel suit, the flannel also covering his face. Short of indicating a prudent change of tailor the incident (if dreams have incidents) serves to point up the temptation to English Kafka and joke him down to size. The Channel is a slipper bath of irony through which we pass these serious continentals in order not to be infected by their gloom. This propensity I am sure I have not escaped or tried to; but then there is something that *is* English about Kafka, and it is not only his self-deprecation. A vegetarian and fond of the sun, he seems a familiar crank; if he'd been living in England at the turn of the century and not in Prague one can imagine him going out hiking and spending evenings with like-minded friends in Letchworth. He is the young man in a Shaw play who strolls past the garden fence in too large shorts to be accosted by some brisk Shavian young woman who, perceiving his charm, takes him in hand, puts paid to his morbid thoughts and makes him pull his socks up.

Charm he certainly had, but not at home. Chewing every mouthful umpteen times so that at meals his father cowered behind the newspaper, Kafka saved his charm for work and for his friends. Home is not the place for charm anyway. We do not look for it around the fireside so it's not so surprising Kafka had no charm for his father. His father, it seems, had none for anybody. There is something called Home Charm though. In the forties it was a kind of distemper and nowadays it's a chain of DIY shops. In that department certainly Kafka did not excel. He was not someone you would ask to help put up a shelf for instance, though one component of his charm was an exaggerated appreciation of people who could, and of commonplace accomplishments generally. Far from being clumsy himself (he had something of the dancer about him) he would marvel (or profess to marvel) at the ease with which other people managed to negotiate the world. This kind of professed incompetence ('Silly me!') often leads to offers of help and carried to extremes it encourages the formation of unofficial protection societies. Thus Kafka was much cosseted by the ladies in his office and in the same way the pupils of another candidate for secular sainthood, the French philosopher Simone Weil, saw to it that their adored teacher did not suffer the consequences of a practical unwisdom even more hopeless than Kafka's.

One cannot say that Kafka's marvelling at mundane accomplishments was not genuine, was a ploy. The snag is that when the person doing the marvelling goes on to do great things this can leave those with the commonplace accomplishments feeling a little flat. Say such a person goes on to win the Nobel Prize it is scant consolation to know that one can change a three-pin plug.

Gorky said that in Chekhov's presence everyone felt a desire to be simpler, more truthful and more oneself. Kafka too had this effect. 'On his entrance into a room', wrote a contemporary, 'it seemed as though some unseen attendant had whispered to the lecturer, "Be careful about everything you say from now on. Franz Kafka has just arrived."' To have this effect on people is a not unmixed blessing. When we are on our best behaviour we are not always at our best.

This is not to say that Kafka did not make jokes in life and in art. *The Trial*, for instance, is a funnier book than it has got credit for and Kafka's jokes about himself are better for the desperate circumstances in which they were often made. He never did win the Nobel Prize of course, but contemplated the possibility once in fun and in pain, and in a fairly restricted category (though one he could have shared with several contemporaries, Proust, Katherine

Mansfield and D. H. Lawrence among them). When he was dying of TB of the larynx he was fetching up a good deal of phlegm. 'I think,' he said (and the joke is more poignant for being so physically painful to make), 'I think I deserve the Nobel Prize for sputum.' Nothing if not sick, it is a joke that could have been made yesterday.

Dead sixty-odd years Kafka is still modern and there is much in the present day world to interest him. These days Kafka would be intrigued by the battery farm and specifically, with an interest both morbid and lively, in the device that de-beaks the still-living chickens; in waste-disposal trucks that chew the rubbish before swallowing it and those dubious restaurants that install for your dining pleasure a tank of doomed trout. As the *maître d'* assists the discerning diner in the ceremony of choice, be aware of the waiter who wields the net: both mourner and executioner, he is Kafka. He notes old people in Zimmer frames stood in their portable dock on perambulatory trial for their lives. He is interested in the feelings of the squash ball and the champagne bottle that launches the ship. In a football match his sympathy is not with either of the teams but with the ball, or, in a match ending nil–nil, with the hunger of the goalmouth. He would be unable to endorse the words of the song by Simon and Garfunkel 'I'd rather be a hammer than a nail', feeling himself (as he confessed to one of his girlfriends) simultaneously both. And in a different context he would be concerned with the current debate on the disposal of nuclear waste. To be placed in a lead canister which is then encased in concrete and sunk fathoms deep to the floor of the ocean was the degree of circulation he thought appropriate for most of his writing. Or not, of course.

Kafka was fond of the cinema and there are short stories, like *Tales of a Red Indian* that have a feeling of the early movies. He died before the talkies came in and so before the Marx Brothers but there is an exchange in *Horse Feathers* that sums up Kafka's relations with his father:

BEPPO: Dad, I'm proud to be your son.

GROUCHO: Son, you took the words out of my mouth. I'm
ashamed to be your father.

The Kafka household could have been the setting for many
Jewish jokes:

FATHER: Son, you hate me.
SON: Father, I love you.
MOTHER: Don't contradict your father.

Had Kafka the father emigrated to America as so many of his contemporaries did, things might have turned out differently for Kafka
the son. He was always stage-struck. Happily lugubrious, he might
have turned out a stand-up Jewish comic. Kafka at Las Vegas.

Why didn't Kafka stutter? The bullying father, the nervous son –
life in the Kafka household seems a blueprint for a speech
impediment. In a sense, of course, he did stutter. Jerky, extruded
with great force and the product of tremendous effort, everything
Kafka wrote is a kind of stutter. Stutterers devise elaborate
routines to avoid or to ambush and take by surprise troublesome
consonants of which K is one of the most difficult. It's a good job
Kafka didn't stutter. With two Ks he might have got started on
his name and never seen the end of it. As it is he docks it, curtails
it, leaves its end behind much as lizards do when something gets
hold of their tail.

In thus de-nominating himself Kafka was to make his name and
his letter memorable. Diminishing it he augmented it and not
merely for posterity. K was a significant letter in his own time.
There were Ks on every banner, palace and official form. Kafka
had two Ks and so in the *Kaiserlich* and *Königlich* of the Habsburg
Emperors, did the Austro-Hungarian Empire. The Emperor at
the time was Franz Joseph and that comes into it too, for here is
Franz K writing about Joseph K in the time of Franz Joseph K.

There was another emperor nearer at hand, the emperor in the
armchair, Kafka's phrase for his father. Hermann Kafka has had

such a consistently bad press that it's hard not to feel a sneaking sympathy for him as for all the Parents of Art. They never get it right. They bring up a child badly and he turns out a writer, posterity never forgives them – though without that unfortunate upbringing the writer might never have written a word. They bring up a child well and he never *does* write a word. Do it right and posterity never hears about the parents; do it wrong and posterity never hears about anything else.

'They fuck you up your Mum and Dad' and if you're planning on writing that's probably a good thing. But if you are planning on writing and they haven't fucked you up, well, you've got nothing to go on, so then they've fucked you up good and proper.

Many parents, one imagines, would echo the words of Madame Weil, the mother of Simone Weil, a child every bit as trying as Kafka must have been. Questioned about her pride in the posthumous fame of her ascetic daughter Madame Weil said, 'Oh! How much I would have preferred her to have been happy.' Like Kafka Simone Weil is often nominated for secular sainthood. I'm not sure. Talk of a saint in the family and there's generally one around if not quite where one's looking. One thinks of Mrs Muggeridge and in the Weil family it is not Simone so much as her mother who consistently behaves well and elicits sympathy. In the Kafka household the halo goes to Kafka's sister Ottla, who has to mediate between father and son, a role in weaker planetary systems than that revolving round Hermann Kafka which is more often played by the mother.

Kafka may have been frightened that he was more like his father than he cared to admit. In a letter to Felice Bauer, Kafka indulges in the fantasy of being a large piece of wood, pressed against the body of a cook 'who is holding the knife along the side of this stiff log (somewhere in the region of my hip) slicing off shavings to light the fire.' Many conclusions could be drawn from this image, some glibber than others. One of them is that Kafka would have liked to have been a chip off the old block.

Daily at his office in the Workers Accident Insurance Institute Kafka was confronted by those unfortunates who had been maimed and injured at work. Kafka was not crippled at work but at home. It's hardly surprising. If a family is a factory for turning out children then it is lacking in the most elementary safety precautions. There are no guard rails round that dangerous engine, the father. There are no safeguards against being scalded by the burning affection of the mother. No mask is proof against the suffocating atmosphere. One should not be surprised that so many lose their balance and are mangled in the machinery of love. Take the Wittgensteins. With three of their five children committing suicide they make the Kafkas seem like a model family. One in Prague, the other in Vienna, Kafka and Wittgenstein often get mentioned in the same breath. Socially they were poles apart but both figure in and are ingredients of the intellectual ferment of the last years of the Austro-Hungarian Empire. Not at all similar in character, Kafka and Wittgenstein sometimes sound alike, as in Wittgenstein's Preface to his *Philosophical Investigations*: 'I make [these remarks] public with doubtful feelings. It is not impossible that it should fall to the lot of this work, in its poverty and in the darkness of this time, to bring light into one brain or another – but, of course, it is not likely. I should not like my writing to spare other people the trouble of thinking. But, if possible, to stimulate someone to thoughts of his own. I should have liked to produce a good book. This has not come about, but the time is past in which I could improve it.'

Though Nabokov was sure he had travelled regularly on the same train as Kafka when they were both in Berlin in 1922, Kafka and Wittgenstein could meet, I suppose, only in the pages of a novel like *Ragtime* or in one of those imaginary encounters (Freud and Kafka is an obvious one) that used to be devised by Maurice Cranston in the days of the BBC Third Programme. But if Wittgenstein had never heard of Kafka, Kafka would certainly have heard of Wittgenstein. It was a noted name in Bohemia where the family owned many steelworks. A steelworks is a dangerous place and the Wittgenstein companies must have contributed their quota to those unfortunates crowding up the steps of the Workers Accident Insurance Institute in Poric Street. So when Kafka did come across the name Wittgenstein it just meant more paperwork.

xiv

It must have been a strange place, the Workers Accident Insurance Institute, a kingdom of the absurd where it did not pay to be well and loss determined gain; limbs became commodities and to be given a clean bill of health was to be sent away empty-handed. There every man carried a price on his head, or on his arm or his leg, like the tariffs of ancient law. It was a world where to be deprived was to be endowed, to be disfigured was to be marked out for reward and to trip was to jump every hurdle. In Kafka's place of work only the whole man had something to hide, the real handicap to have no handicap at all, whereas a genuine limp genuinely acquired cleared every obstacle and a helping hand was one that had first been severed from the body. The world as hospital, it is Nietzsche's nightmare.

Kafka's career in insurance coincides with the period when compensation for injury at work is beginning to be accepted as a necessary condition of employment. Workers' compensation was and is a pretty unmixed blessing but it did spawn a new disease – or at any rate a new neurosis. Did one want a neurosis, the turn of the century in Austro-Hungary was the time and place to have it, except that this condition was a product of the factory not the drawing room, not so richly upholstered or so literate or capable of literature as those articulate fantasies teased out at No. 19 Berggasse. Compensation neurosis is a condition that affected and affects those (they tend to be women more than men) who have suffered a slight accident at work, and in particular an accident to the head: a slight bump, say, a mild concussion, nothing significant. Before the introduction of compensation such a minor mishap was likely to be ignored or forgotten. With no chance of compensation there was no incidence of neurosis, grin and bear it the order of the day. But once there is the possibility of compensation (and if the – scarcely – injured party does not know this there will be well-wishers who will tell him or her) then the idea is planted that he or she might be owed something. One does not need to be a conscious malingerer to feel that some recompense is perhaps called for, and from this feeling is bred dissatisfaction, headaches, wakefulness, the whole cabinet of neurotic symptoms.

With Lily in *The Insurance Man* I have assumed that such a case did occasionally get as far as the Workers Accident Insurance Institute. If so then here was one more hopeless quest going on round the corridors of that unhappy building. This kind of quest, where what is wanted is the name of the illness as well as compensation for it, has something in common with Joseph K's quest in *The Trial*. He wants his offence identified but no one will give it a name; this is his complaint. Until his offence is named he cannot find a tribunal to acquit him of it.

Kafka and Proust both begin on the frontiers of dreams. It is in the gap between sleeping and waking where Marcel is trying to place his surroundings that Gregor Samsa finds himself transformed into a beetle and Joseph K finds himself under arrest. *Metamorphosis* and *The Trial* are the two works of Kafka that are best known, are, if you like, classics. Classics – and in particular modern classics – are the books one thinks one ought to read, thinks one has read. In this category particularly for readers who were young in the fifties come Proust, Sartre, Orwell, Camus and Kafka. It isn't simply a matter of pretension. As a young man I genuinely felt I ought to read Proust and Eliot (though it did no harm to be seen reading them). However, a few pages convinced me that I had got the gist and so they went on to the still uncluttered bookshelf beside Kafka, Camus, Orwell and the rest.

The theory these days (or one of them) is that the reader brings as much to the book as the author. So how much more do readers bring who have never managed to get through the book at all? It follows that the books one remembers best are the books one has never read. To be remembered but not read has been the fate of *The Trial* despite it being the most readable of Kafka's books. Kafka on the whole is not very readable. But then to be readable does not help a classic. Great books are taken as read, or taken as having been read. If they are read, or read too often and too easily by too many, the likelihood is they are not great books or won't remain so for long. Read too much they crumble away as nowadays popular mountains are prone to do.

The readers or non-readers of *The Trial* remember it wrong. Its reputation is as a tale about man and bureaucracy, a fable appropriate to the office block. One recalls the office in Orson

Welles's film – a vast hangar in which hundreds of clerks toil at identical desks to an identical routine. In fact *The Trial* is set in small rooms in dark houses in surroundings that are picturesque, romantic and downright quaint. For the setting of *The Trial* there is no blaming the planners. It is all on an impeccably human scale.

The topography that oppressed Kafka does not oppress us. Kafka's fearful universe is constructed out of burrows and garrets and cubby-holes on back staircases. It is nearer to Dickens and *Alice* and even to the cosiness of *The Wind in the Willows* than it is to our own particular emptinesses. Our shorthand for desolation is quite different: the assembly line, the fence festooned with polythene rags, the dead land between the legs of the motorway. But it is ours. It isn't Kafka's. Or, to put it another way, the trouble with Kafka is that he didn't know the word Kafkaesque. However, those who see *The Trial* as a trailer for totalitarian bureaucracy might be confirmed in this view on finding that the premises in Dzherzhinsky Square in Moscow now occupied by the Lubianka Prison formerly housed another institution, the Rossiya Insurance Company.

Joseph K's first examination takes place one Sunday morning in Juliusstrasse, a shabby street of poor tenements. The address he had been given was of a gaunt apartment building with a vast entrance that led directly into a courtyard formed by many storeys of tenement flats.

Futile to go looking for that courtyard in Prague today. It exists after all only in the mind of a dead author whom you may not even have read. But say you did go looking for it, as a Proust reader might go looking for Combray, or Brontë fans for Wuthering Heights and say even that you found the address, it still would not be as Kafka or as Joseph K describes it. These days the stone would have been scrubbed, the brick pointed, the mouldings given back their old (which is to say their new) sharpness in what the hoarding on the site advertises as a government-assisted programme of restoration and refurbishment. Go where you like in the old quarters of Europe it is the same. Decay has been arrested, the cracks filled; in Padua, Perpignan and Prague urban dentistry has triumphed.

The setting for Joseph K's first examination is a small room with a low ceiling, a kind of upstairs basement, a rooftop cellar. It is a location he finds only with difficulty since it can be reached only through the kitchen of one of the apartments. It is this block of apartments, let us imagine, that has now been restored, the architect of which, grey hair, young face, bright tie and liberal up to a point (architects, like dentists, being the same the world over) here shows off his latest piece of conservation:

What we had here originally was a pretty rundown apartment building. The tenants, many of whom had lived here literally for generations, were mainly in the lower-income bracket – joiners, cleaners, factory workers and so on, plus some single ladies who were probably no better than they should be. I believe the whole district was rather famous for that actually. My problem was how to do justice to the building, improve the accommodation while (single ladies apart) hanging on to some sort of social mix.

Stage 1 involved getting possession of the building itself, which, since it's situated in the heart of the conservation area, we were able to do by means of a government grant. Stage 2 was to empty the apartments. Happily many of the tenants were elderly so we could leave this largely to a process of natural wastage. When the overall population of the building had come down to a manageable number, Stage 3 involved locating this remnant in local-authority housing on the outskirts. Which brings us to Stage 4, the restoration and refurbishment of the building itself.

Initially what we did was to divide it up into a number of two- and three-bedroom units, targeted, I suppose, on lawyers, architects, communications people, the kind of tenant who still finds the demands of urban living quite stimulating. We've got one or two studios on the top floor for artists of one kind and another, photographers and so on, and a similar number of old people on the ground floor. Actually we were obliged to include those under the terms of the government grant but though they do take up some very desirable space, I actually welcome them. A building of this kind is after all a community, old, young – variety is of the essence.

The particular unit associated with the gentleman in the novel is on the fifth floor. Trudge, trudge, trudge. I'm afraid the lifts are still unconnected. Bureaucracy, the workings of.

And so they go upstairs to the fifth floor as Joseph K went up that Sunday morning in the novel, looking for the room where his examination was set to take place.

'Actually I remember this particular apartment,' says the architect, 'because it was a bit of an odd one out. Whereas most of the other flats amalgamated quite nicely into two- and three-bedroomed units, this particular one wouldn't fit into any of our categories. Here we are. You come into a small room, you see which has obviously served as a kitchen . . . '

'Yes,' says the visitor. 'That's described in the book.'

'Never read it alas,' says the architect. 'Work, pressure of. Come in, have supper, slump in front of the old telly box and that's it for the night. However, this kitchen rather unexpectedly opens into this much larger room. Two windows, rather nicely proportioned and I think once upon a time there must have been a platform at the far end.'

'Yes,' says the visitor. 'That's in the book too.'

'And does he mention this?' asks the architect. 'This rather attractive feature, the gallery running round under the ceiling?'

'Yes,' says the visitor. 'People sat up there during his examination. They were rather cramped. In fact they were so cramped they had to bend double with cushions between their backs and the ceiling.'

'Is that in the book?' asks the architect.

'Yes. It's all in the book,' says the visitor.

'Really,' says the architect. 'It sounds jollier than I thought. I thought it was some frightful political thing. Anyway we had a site conference and all of us – architects, rental agents and prospective tenants agreed it would be a great pity to lose the gallery. Someone suggested converting the place into a studio with the gallery as a kind of sleeping area but that smacked a little bit of alternative life-styles which we were quite anxious to avoid, so in the end we've given it a lick of paint and just left it, the upshot being that the management are probably going to donate the room to the tenants. If it has some connection with this fellow in the novel perhaps we could call it after him.'

'The Joseph K room,' says the visitor. 'But what would you use it for?'

'Well, what will we use it for?' says the architect. 'I don't want to use the dread words "community centre" with all the overtones of Bingo and Saturday night hop. But it could be used for all sorts. As soon as you say the word "crèche", for instance, you've got the ladies on your side. Encounter groups and suchlike, keep-fit classes, and then, of course, we have the Residents' Association. What we are hoping you see is that the residents will *join in*. After all this is a co-operative. Everybody needs to pull their weight and to that end all the tenants have been carefully – I was going to say screened, but let's say we've made a few preliminary enquiries in terms of background, outlook and so on, nothing so vulgar as vetting, you understand, but if we are all going to be neighbours it makes for less trouble in the long run.

'And supposing anybody does step out of line, stereo going full blast in the wee small hours, ladies coming up and down a little too often (or indeed gentlemen in this day and age) kiddies making a mess on the stairs, then in that event I think this room would be the ideal place for the culprit to be interviewed by the Residents' Association, asked to be a little more considerate and even see the error of their ways. After all I think a line has to be drawn somewhere. And the Joseph K Memorial Room would be just the place to do it.'

In our cosy little island, novel readers must seldom be accused of crimes they did not commit, or crimes of any sort for that matter: PROUST READER ON BURGLARY RAP is not a headline that carries conviction. Few of us are likely to be arrested without charge or expect to wake up and find the police in the room, and our experience of bureaucracy comes not from the Gestapo so much as from the Gas Board. So *The Trial* does not at first sight seem like a book to be read with dawning recognition, the kind of book one looks up from and says, 'But it's my story!'

Nor is it a book for the sick room and seldom to be found on those trolleys of literary jumble trundled round the wards of local hospitals every Wednesday afternoon by Miss Venables, the voluntary worker. The book trolley and the food trolley are not dissimilar, hospital reading and hospital food both lacking taste and substance and neither having much in the way of roughage. The guardian and conductress of the book trolley, Miss Venables, seldom reads herself and would have been happier taking round the tea, for which the patients are more grateful and less choosy than they are over the books. But in the absence of a Mr Venables and because she has no figure to speak of, Miss Venables is generally taken to be rather refined and thus has got landed with literature. The real life sentences come from judgements on our personal appearance and good behaviour, far from remitting the sentence, simply confirms it and makes it lifelong. Kafka was always delicate and his father therefore assumed he was a book-worm, an assumption his son felt was unwarranted and which he vigorously denied.

Miss Venables is not a bookworm either, seldom venturing inside the books she purveys, which she judges solely by their titles. Most patients, she thinks, want to be taken out of them-selves, particularly so in Surgical. In Surgical novels are a form of homeopathy: having had something taken out of themselves the patients now want something else to take them out of themselves. So coming out of Surgical Miss Venables finds her stock of novels running pretty low as she pauses now in Admissions at the bedside of a patient who has come in, as he has been told, 'just for observation'. Presumptuous to call him Mr Kay, let us call him Mr Jay.

'Fiction or non-fiction?' asks Miss Venables.

'Fiction,' says Mr Jay, and hopes he is going to do better than last week. Last week he had wanted a copy of *Jake's Thing*, but could not remember the title and had finished up with *Howards End*.

'Fiction,' says Miss Venables (who would have come in handy in the Trinitarian controversy), 'Fiction is divided into Fiction, Mystery and Romance. Which would you like?'

Truthfully Mr Jay wants a tale of sun and lust but daunted by

Miss Venables's unprepossessing appearance he lamely opts for Mystery. She gives him a copy of *The Trial*.

How *The Trial* comes to be classified under Mystery is less of a mystery than how it comes to be on the trolley at all. In fact it had originally formed part of the contents of the locker of a deceased lecturer in Modern Languages and had been donated to the hospital library by his grateful widow, along with his copy of Thomas Mann's *Magic Mountain*. This Miss Venables has classified under Children and Fairy Stories. So leaving Mr Jay leafing listlessly through Kafka she passes on with her trolley to other wards and other disappointments.

It does not take Mr Jay long to realize that he has picked another dud, and one even harder to read than *Howards End*. What is to be made of such sentences as 'The verdict doesn't come all at once; the proceedings gradually merge into the verdict.'? Mr Jay has a headache. He puts *The Trial* on his locker beside the bottle of Lucozade and the Get Well cards and tries to sleep, but can't. Instead he settles back and thinks about his body. These days he thinks about little else. The surgeon Mr McIver has told him he is a mystery. Matron says he has baffled the doctors. So Mr Jay feels like somebody special. Now they come for him and he is carefully manoeuvred under vast machines by aproned figures, who then discreetly retire. Later, returned to his bed, he tries again to read but feels so sick he cannot read his book even if he really wanted to. And that is a pity. Because Mr Jay might now begin to perceive that *The Trial* is not a mystery story and that it is not particularly about the law or bureaucracy or any of the things the editor's note says it is about. It is about something nearer home, and had he come once again upon the sentence 'The verdict doesn't come all at once; the proceedings gradually merge into the verdict' Mr Jay might have realized that Kafka is talking to him. It *is* his story.

In the short story *Metamorphosis* Gregor Samsa wakes up as a beetle. Nabokov, who knew about beetles, poured scorn on those who translated or depicted the insectified hero as a cockroach. Kafka did not want the beetle depicted at all but for the error of classification he is largely to blame. It was Kafka who first brought up the subject of cockroaches though in a different story, *Wedding Preparations in the Country*. 'I have, as I lie in bed,' he writes, 'the form of a large beetle, a stag beetle or a cockchafer, I believe.' Cockroach or not, Gregor Samsa has become so famous waking up as a beetle I am surprised he has not been taken up and metamorphosed again, this time by the advertising industry. Since he wakes up as a beetle why should he not wake up as a Volkswagen? Only this time he's not miserable but happy. And so of course is his family. Why not? They've got themselves a nice little car. The only problem is how to get it out of the bedroom.

The first biography of Kafka was written by his friend and editor Max Brod. It was Brod who rescued Kafka's works from oblivion, preserved them and, despite Kafka's instructions to the contrary, published them after his death. Brod, who was a year younger than Kafka (though one somehow thinks of him as older) lived on until 1968. The author of innumerable essays and articles, Brod published some eighty-three books, one for every year of his life. Described in *The Times* obituary as 'himself an author of uncommonly versatile stamp' he turned out novels at regular intervals until the end of his life, the last one being set during the Arab–Israeli war. These novels fared poorly with the critics and were one able to collect the reviews of his books one would find few, I imagine, that do not somewhere invoke the name of Kafka, with the comparison inevitably to Brod's disadvantage. This cannot have been easy to take. He who had erected not only Kafka's monument but created his reputation never managed to struggle out of its shadow. He could be forgiven if he came to be as dubious of Kafka's name as Kafka was himself.

Never quite Kafka's wife, after Kafka's death Brod's role was that of the devoted widow, standing guard over the reputation, authorizing the editions, editing the diaries and driving trespassers from the grave. However, living in Tel Aviv, he was spared the fate of equivalent figures in English culture, an endless round of arts programmes where those who have known the famous are publicly debriefed of their memories, knowing as their own dusk falls that they will be remembered only for remembering someone else.

Kafka was a minor executive in an insurance company in Prague. In *Kafka's Dick* this fact is picked up by another minor executive in another insurance firm, but in Leeds seventy-odd years later. Sydney, as the insurance man, decides to do a piece on Kafka for an insurance periodical (I imagine there are such, though I've never verified the fact). As he works on his piece Sydney comes to resent his subject, as biographers must often do. Biographers are only fans after all, and fans have been known to shoot their idols.

'Why biography?' asks his wife.

Sydney's answer is less of a speech than an aria, which is probably why it was cut from the play:

I want to hear about the shortcomings of great men, their fears and their failings. I've had enough of their vision, how they altered the landscape (we stand on their shoulders to survey our lives). So. Let's talk about the vanity. Read how this one, the century's seer, increases his stature by lifts in his shoes. That one, the connoisseur of emptiness, is tipped for the Nobel Prize yet still needs to win at Monopoly. This playwright's skin is so thin he can feel pain on the other side of the world. So why is he deaf to the suffering next door; signs letters to the newspapers but holds his own wife a prisoner of conscience? The slipshod poet keeps immaculate time and expects it of everyone else, but never wears underwear and frequently smells. That's not important, of course, but what is? The gentle novelist's frightful temper, the Christian poet's mad, unvisited wife, the hush in their households where the dog goes on tiptoe, meals on the dot at their ironclad whim? Note with these great men the flight and not infrequent suicide of their children, their brisk remarriage on the deaths of irreplaceable wives. Proud of his modesty one gives frequent, rare interviews in which he aggregates praise and denudes others of credit. Indifferent to the lives about him he considers his day ruined on finding a slighting reference to himself in a periodical published three years ago in New Zealand. And demands sympathy from his family on that account. And gets it. Our father the novelist, my husband the poet. He belongs to the ages, just don't catch him at breakfast. Artists, celebrated for their humanity, they turn out to be scarcely human at all.

Death took no chances with Kafka and laid three traps for his life. Parched and voiceless from TB of the larynx, he was forty, the victim, as he himself said, of a conspiracy by his own body. But had his lungs not ganged up on him there was a second trap, twenty years down the line when the agents of death would have shunted him, as they did his three sisters, into the gas chambers. That fate, though it was not to be his, is evident in his last photograph. It is a face that prefigures the concentration camp.

But say that in 1924 he cheats death and a spell in the sanatorium restores him to health. In 1938 he sees what is coming – Kafka after all was more canny than he is given credit for, not least by Kafka himself – and so he slips away from Prague in time. J. P. Stern imagines him fighting with the partisans; Philip Roth finds him a poor teacher of Hebrew in Newark, New Jersey. Whatever his future when he leaves Prague he becomes what he has always been, a refugee. Maybe (for there is no harm in dreams) he even lives long enough to find himself the great man he never knew he was. Maybe (the most impossible dream of all) he actually succeeds in putting on weight. So where is death now? Waiting for Kafka in some Park Avenue consulting room where he goes with what he takes to be a recurrence of his old chest complaint.

'Quite curable now, of course. TB. No problem. However, regarding your chest you say you managed a factory once?'

'Yes. For my brother-in-law. For three or four years.'

'When was that?'

'A long time ago. It closed in 1917. In Prague.'

'What kind of factory was it?'

'Building materials. Asbestos.'

This is just a dream of Kafka's death. He is famous, the owner of the best-known initial in literature and we know he did not die like this. Others probably did. In Prague the consulting rooms are bleaker but the disease is the same and the treatment as futile. These patients have no names, though Kafka would have known them, those girls (old ladies now) whom he describes brushing the thick asbestos dust from their overalls, the casualties of his brother-in-law's ill-starred business in which Hermann, his father, had invested. A good job his father isn't alive, the past master of 'I told you so'.

In the last weeks of his life Kafka was taken to a sanatorium in the Wienerwald and here, where the secret of dreams had been revealed to Freud, Kafka's dreams ended.

On the window sill the night before he died Dora Dymant found an owl waiting. The owl has a complex imagery in art. Just as in Freudian psychology an emotion can stand for itself and its opposite, so is the owl a symbol of both darkness and light. As a creature of the night the owl was seen as a symbol of the Jews who, turning away from the light of Christ, were guilty of wilful blindness. On the other hand the owl was, as it remains, a symbol of wisdom. It is fitting that this bird of ambiguity should come to witness the departure of a man who by belief was neither Christian nor Jew, and who had never wholeheartedly felt himself a member of the human race. He had written of himself as a bug and a mouse, both the natural prey of the bird now waiting outside the window.

KAFKA'S DICK

CHARACTERS

KAFKA
BROD
LINDA
FATHER
SYDNEY
HERMANN K
JULIE

Kafka's Dick was first performed at the Royal Court Theatre, London, on 23 September 1986. The cast was as follows:

KAFKA	Roger Lloyd Pack
BROD	Andrew Sachs
LINDA	Alison Steadman
FATHER	Charles Lamb
SYDNEY	Geoffrey Palmer
HERMANN K	Jim Broadbent
JULIE	Vivian Pickles

Director	Richard Eyre
Designer	William Dudley
Lighting Designer	Mark Henderson
Sound	Christopher Shutt
Music, Effects and Arrangements	George Fenton
Dances	David Toguri

ACT ONE

SCENE ONE

The date is immaterial, though it is around 1919. KAFKA, *a tall, good-looking man is sitting in a chair, dying.* MAX BROD, *his friend, is smaller, slightly hump-backed, and very much alive.*

KAFKA: Max.

BROD: I hoped you were sleeping.

KAFKA: Max.

(*Pause.*)

BROD: What?

KAFKA: I think I shall die soon.

(BROD *says nothing.*)

Did you hear me, Max?

BROD: Let's cross that bridge when you come to it. You've said you were dying before.

KAFKA: I know. But I won't let you down this time, I promise.

BROD: Kafka, I want you to *live*.

KAFKA: Forgive me. If I die . . .

BROD: What's this if? He says he's dying then suddenly it's 'if'. Don't you mean 'when'?

KAFKA: When I die I want you to do me a favour.

BROD: Come to the funeral, you mean? Look, this is Max, your best friend. I'll be up there in the front row.

KAFKA: No. The funeral can take care of itself.

BROD: Pardon me for saying so, but that's typical of your whole attitude to life. A funeral does not take care of itself.

KAFKA: (*Overlapping*) I know, Max. I know.

BROD: Take the eats for a start. You're dealing with grief-stricken people. They want to be able to weep secure in the knowledge that once you're in the grave the least they'll be offered will be a choice of sandwiches.

KAFKA: But after the funeral . . . this is very important . . . I want you to promise me something, Max. You must burn everything I've ever written.

5

BROD: No.

KAFKA: Stories, novels, letters. Everything.

BROD: What about the royalties?

KAFKA: I've published one novel and a few short stories. Does it matter?

BROD: But where would they go in a bereavement situation?

KAFKA: My father, where else? Which is another reason to burn them. I've got stuff in technical periodicals to do with my work at the insurance company. Don't worry about that . . .

BROD: But the rest I burn, right?

KAFKA: Yes.

BROD: That is your honest decision?

KAFKA: Cross my heart and hope to die.

BROD: That's not saying much; you are going to die.

KAFKA: Max, I *mean* it. All my works burned. Understand?

BROD: All your works burned.

KAFKA: Everything. When I go, they go. Finish.

BROD: You've got it. Message received and understood.
(*Pause.*)

KAFKA: Where are you going?

BROD: To buy paraffin.

KAFKA: Max. Stay a minute. After all, my writings are worthless. They wouldn't survive anyway. They don't deserve to survive.
(*Pause.*)
Don't you think so?

BROD: You're the one who's dying. I'm Max, your faithful friend. You say burn them, I burn them. (*Going again*) Maybe I'll get petrol instead.

KAFKA: Max! (*Pause.*) If you want to read them first, feel free . . . just to remind you.

BROD: (*Going again*) No. I read them when you wrote them. If I'm going to burn them I may as well press on and burn them. Only . . .

KAFKA: (*Brightening*) What?

BROD: Well, I ask myself, are we missing an opportunity here? Why not juice up the occasion? . . . Ask one or two people over, split a bottle of vino, barbecue the odd steak then as a

climax to the proceedings flambé the Collected Works?
Anyway, old friend, don't worry. All will be taken care of.

KAFKA: Good. Still, if in fact you can't get hold of all my stuff, no
matter. Some of it has been published. It could be anywhere.

BROD: You're kidding. I mean, what are we saying here? This is
your faithful friend, Max. Kafka wants his stuff burned,
Max will find it and burn it. It won't be difficult. You'd be
surprised how helpful people are when it's a dying wish.

KAFKA: But I'm in libraries, Max. You can't burn them.
Metamorphosis, my story about a man who wakes up as a
beetle. That's in libraries. Ah well. I shall just have to live
with that.

BROD: Don't be so negative. Here's the plan. I go to the library,
borrow your books, go back and say they've been stolen.
Then it's burn, baby, burn.

KAFKA: Some are in America. London. Paris.

BROD: So? I've always wanted an excuse to travel. I can't wait.
Max Brod. Search and destroy! (*Pause.*) Hey, you look really
depressed.

KAFKA: Wouldn't you be depressed? I'm dying.
(*Pause.*)

BROD: Look. *Vis-à-vis* your books. I've just had a thought.

KAFKA: (*Clutching at a straw*) Yes?

BROD: Maybe I won't burn everything. Not every single copy.
Could you live with that?

KAFKA: Well . . . I . . . I'm not sure. I really wanted them
burnt . . .

BROD: Can I just let you in on my thinking? We're in 1920 now,
right? You're going to die soon . . . give a year, take a year,
say 1924 at the outside. Well, less than ten years later we get
the Nazis, right? And, as prefigured in some of your as yet
unrecognized masterpieces (which I'm going to burn, I
know, I know), the Nazis seize power and put into operation
the full apparatus of totalitarian bureaucracy.

KAFKA: Max, I saw it coming.

BROD: You did.

KAFKA: Would that history had proved me wrong, Max.

BROD: Would that it had. Only, tragically it didn't. Because in

1933 the Nazis are scheduled to stage their infamous Burning
of the Books . . .

KAFKA: Burn books? Who in his right mind would want to burn
books? They must be sick.

BROD: The Nazis ransack libraries for what they term decadent
literature. Film shows Brownshirts bringing out books by
the armful and casting them into the flames.

KAFKA: In civilized Europe! I can't bear it. It's tragic. It's insane.
(*Pause.*) Max. Which books in particular?

BROD: Freud. Proust. Rilke. Brecht.

KAFKA: Er . . . anybody else?

BROD: Hemingway. Thomas Mann. Gide. Joyce . . .

KAFKA: Max . . . Don't I figure?

BROD: Well, this is the point . . . I'll have burnt your stuff
already.

KAFKA: But nobody will know that.

BROD: Exactly. People will look at the credits and say: They
burnt Proust. They burnt Brecht. They burnt Joyce. Where
is Kafka? Not worth burning, maybe.

KAFKA: God. I was depressed before. Now I'm suicidal.

BROD: Maybe I can fix it.

KAFKA: You think?

BROD: I can see it now: a shot of flames licking round a book
jacket, the name Kafka prominently placed.

KAFKA: Dreadful.

BROD: Sure, but burn one and you sell ten thousand. Believe
me, if the Nazis hadn't thought of it the publishers would.

KAFKA: Max, I'm still not sure. Do I want to survive?

BROD: Of course you do. I'm a successful novelist, so I'm headed
that way myself. I know you've got talent. You haven't made
it big yet, in fact you haven't made it at all, but once you're
dead I've got a hunch your fame is going to snowball. Who
knows, you could end up as famous as me. Whereas, you
burn everything, you've squandered your life.

KAFKA: You're right.

BROD: Believe me, in ten years' time, your stuff is going to be
classic. That one you mentioned, *Metamorphosis*, where he
wakes up one morning and finds he's a cockroach. Brilliant.

8

KAFKA: (*Leaping from his chair*) That's it. That is *it*. I've changed my mind. As you were. Burn them. Burn everything!

BROD: What did I say?

KAFKA: What did you *say*? What did you say? He didn't wake up as a cockroach. I never said he woke up as a cockroach. He woke up as a beetle.

BROD: Cockroach, beetle, they're both bugs, who cares?

KAFKA: Me! Don't you see? That's the trouble with words. You write one thing, the reader makes it into another. You try to be honest, only words fail you. They always do in the end. They're the worst method of communicating with anybody.

BROD: Look . . .

KAFKA: No, I was right first time. Burn them.

BROD: If you say so.

KAFKA: And Max. No biography.

BROD: Who'll want to write your biography? You won't have written anything.

KAFKA: Promise.

BROD: I promise.

KAFKA: Forgive me. I'm a terrible human being.

BROD: Don't worry about it. (*Yawns.*)

KAFKA: I'm just a dog pretending to be a person, an ape.

BROD: Yeah, yeah. We've been through all that. Now try and sleep a little. Come to bed.

(*The lights begin to fade, with music possibly.*)

KAFKA: I would sleep, only I dream.

BROD: Everybody dreams.

KAFKA: Not like me. I dream the future.

(*Lights up on next scene as soon as* KAFKA *and* BROD *are off.*)

SCENE TWO

The present day. A room in a middle-class house, possibly a kitchen-cum-living room. I am not sure how representational the room should be. Since some of the happenings that take place in it are downright unreal perhaps the room should look unreal also, but the reverse could be more convincingly argued. An over-scrupulous naturalism would be

9

out of place, though the reality of the bookcase is crucial. There are doors or exits to other parts of the house, and an entrance, nay, french windows on to the garden.

SYDNEY, *a mild middle-aged man, is reading.* LINDA, *his wife, stares out into the garden. Sydney's* FATHER, *an old man with a Zimmer frame, is consulting the bookcase.*

LINDA: That fool of a tortoise is out again. Galloping across the lawn.

FATHER: When are they coming?

LINDA: (*Ignoring him but without rancour*) They are not coming.

FATHER: (*Taking an orange Penguin paperback from the bookcase and carrying it over to* LINDA) Is that a detective?

LINDA: (*Still ignoring him*) There are no detectives. Nobody is coming.

FATHER: What have I done?

SYDNEY: (*Kindly*) Nothing, Father. You have done nothing. (*Pause.*) There can be few people who realize that Hitler went to the same school as Wittgenstein.

LINDA: The way he went on to behave I'm surprised he went to school at all.

SYDNEY: Another five years they might have been sharing the same desk.

LINDA: You are clever, Sydney.

FATHER: (*Now poised to leave*) When are they coming?

LINDA: They are not coming.

(FATHER *exits.*)

When are they coming?

SYDNEY: They didn't say.

(*He looks unhappy.*)

LINDA: Now it's making a beeline for the road. It must want to die.

SYDNEY: I wonder if there was a school magazine. Old Boys' Notes. Wittgenstein, L. (Class of 1904) has just published his *Tractatus Logico-Philosophicus* and been elected a Fellow of Trinity College, Cambridge. Contemporaries will recall the model sewing machine he made out of matchsticks. Hitler, A. (Class of 1899) has recently been elected

Chancellor of Germany. He will be remembered as an enthusiastic secretary of the Art Group.

LINDA: Does Mr Cunliffe read?

SYDNEY: I don't know. As Deputy Supervisor Vehicle Insurance North Western Area I doubt if he gets much chance.

(LINDA *says nothing*.)

I didn't want the job. And remember this: Mr Cunliffe has never had an article in the *Journal of Insurance Studies*.

LINDA: No, but Mrs Cunliffe's got a new bedroom suite and they pop over to Jersey quite regularly. (*Pause*.) Why do you never read novels?

SYDNEY: I'm an insurance man, I prefer facts. Biography. I'd rather read about writers than read what they write.

LINDA: Yes. I know why. More dirt.

SYDNEY: (*At the bookcase*) Not necessarily. *The Life of E. M. Forster*. Hardly dirt.

LINDA: Really? I thought he lived with a policeman.

SYDNEY: He was a friend. Forster had friends in many walks of life.

LINDA: Not merely walks. You said one was an Egyptian tram-driver. And there were umpteen darkies.

SYDNEY: Linda. (*Pause*.) We complain about my father: Kafka's father used to rummage in his ears with a toothpick then use it to pick his teeth.

(*She hangs over his shoulder, looking at his books. She would probably like to be in bed.*)

LINDA: No pictures?

SYDNEY: No. I sometimes wish biographies carried nude photographs.

LINDA: Sydney.

SYDNEY: It would settle this argument anyway. (*Holds up a book*.) This is by two psychologists at the University of North Carolina, who, having analysed everything Kafka ever wrote, deduce that one of his problems, of which there were many, was a small penis.

LINDA: I never liked the word penis. I don't mind the pee . . . after all that's what it's for. It's the –nis I somehow don't like. Anyway, he's not unique in that department.

SYDNEY: Linda.

LINDA: I was thinking of Scott Fitzgerald.

SYDNEY: How do you know Scott Fitzgerald had a small . . . thing?

LINDA: The same way I know W. H. Auden never wore underpants, that Kafka's grandfather could pick up a sack of potatoes in his teeth and that Kafka's father used to rummage in his ears with a toothpick. Because that kind of conversation is all I ever get. If it weren't for looking after your father I could still be a nurse.

SYDNEY: I like odd facts.

LINDA: When are you going to tell me the bits in between? I'd thought of taking a course. So I can help you in your work.

SYDNEY: An insurance course?

LINDA: This work.

SYDNEY: If there are courses in Kafka, which I doubt, they would be the first casualty of cutbacks.

LINDA: Literature in general.

SYDNEY: Ah. Literature in general.

LINDA: I should have stayed a nurse. What do I do now? Hang about. I'm nothing.

SYDNEY: I know it's a wicked thing to say nowadays but you are not nothing. You are my wife.

LINDA: It's not enough.

SYDNEY: It's enough for Mrs Cunliffe.

LINDA: Couldn't I do research? File your papers?
(*She makes a move to do so. He stops her.*)

SYDNEY: Linda.

LINDA: Let me at least read it.

SYDNEY: (*Taking back his manuscript*) You wouldn't understand it.

LINDA: I might. After all he's got a nice face. Would I have liked him?

SYDNEY: He was never short of symptoms. You could at least have nursed him. You wouldn't like his stories. Not what you'd call 'true to life'. A man turns into a cockroach. An ape lectures. Mice talk. He'd like me. We've got so much in

12

common. He was in insurance. I'm in insurance. He had TB. I had TB. He didn't like his name. I don't like my name. I'm sure the only reason I drifted into insurance was because I was called Sydney.

LINDA: Sydney's a nice name. I like Sydney.

SYDNEY: Now this is interesting. Kafka had read *Crime and Punishment*, which is a novel by Dostoevsky. In *Crime and Punishment* the student Raskolnikov commits a murder for which another man is wrongly arrested; the man is a house painter. In Kafka's *The Trial*, Joseph K is wrongly arrested. Who has actually committed the crime? A house painter. And someone in whose name millions of people were wrongly arrested was Adolf Hitler. Who is himself wrongly accused of being . . . a house painter.

(*Pause.*)

LINDA: And?

SYDNEY: Linda, it's interesting.

LINDA: It is, it is.

SYDNEY: One of the functions of literary criticism is to point up unexpected connections.

LINDA: With you being in accident insurance I thought your only interest in unexpected connections was when they occurred between motor cars. Sydney.

(*She draws him out of the chair.*)

SYDNEY: Linda. It's 2.30 in the afternoon.

LINDA: It'll be another unexpected connection.

(*The doorbell goes. They stop.*)

SYDNEY: Is his case packed?

(LINDA *nods.*)

LINDA: Sydney (*meaning 'Be brave'*).

(LINDA *answers the door, but the visitor has already come round to the french windows. It is* BROD, *who is just as we have seen him previously, except that he is minus his hump. He carries in his hand a large Homburg hat.*)

BROD: I ring your doorbell with reluctance. I have met with an accident. I am a visitor to these shores. Suddenly a temperamental prostate and a total absence of toilet facilities necessitates my emptying my bladder outside your front door.

13

LINDA: (*Returning*) Sydney, it's all over the step.

BROD: Worse is to follow. Picture my distress as I am rebuttoning
   my trousers when I discover I have urinated not only over
   your doorstep but also over your tortoise.
   (*He removes the Homburg hat revealing the tortoise.*)

LINDA: Our tortoise? (*Puts out her hand for the tortoise then thinks
   better of it.*) He's wet through!
   (BROD *puts the tortoise down on the floor. It begins to move off –*
   BROD, *without looking, puts his Homburg hat over it.*)

SYDNEY: It was an accident, I'm sure.

BROD: Blame the disappearance of your public conveniences.
   Time was they were the envy of the civilized world. To be
   incontinent here is some problem, I can tell you.
   (*The doorbell has alerted* FATHER *and he has come in.*)

FATHER: It's not true. Someone's been telling lies about me. I
   am not incontinent. Furthermore I can tell you the name of
   the Prime Minister. Are you them?

SYDNEY: No, he is not them. There is no them. This gentleman
   has just urinated over the tortoise.

FATHER: I know what that means. You want my room.

BROD: Why does my urinating over the tortoise mean they want
   your room?

SYDNEY: My father imagines things.

FATHER: I don't imagine things. You say I imagine things. I
   never imagine things.
   (*At which point Brod's hat begins to move slowly across the room
   towards* FATHER, *who retreats before it in shocked silence, then
   (Zimmer frame permitting) bolts.* LINDA *picks up the hat and hands
   it to* BROD. *Ignoring the cue to go he sits down and opens a book.*)

SYDNEY: Should we offer him a cup of tea?

LINDA: And put another innocent tortoise at risk? No.

BROD: How singular! I open a book and what do I find? Kafka.
   (*Opening others*) Kafka, Kafka.

SYDNEY: You know his work?

BROD: Only by heart. 'As Gregor Samsa awoke one morning from
   uneasy dreams he found himself transformed into a gigantic
   cockroach.' 'Ah, ha,' says the browser at the airport bookstall.
   'The very thing to while away my flight to Sri Lanka.' And

14

ring a ding ding. It's another sale for our Czech Chekhov.

LINDA: I was a nurse. Waking up people was half my job. I never came across anyone waking up as an insect.

BROD: You probably never came across metaphor either. She says no one wakes up as a cockroach. Next to her I'd wake up a wild beast. So what is it about our Prague Proust that interests you?

SYDNEY: It's not generally known but Kafka worked all his life in an insurance office . . .

BROD: It is known to some people.

SYDNEY: And as I'm in that line myself, I'm writing a piece about him for *Small Print*, the Journal of Insurance Studies.

BROD: For a moment I thought you were yet another of those academic blow flies who make a living buzzing round the faeces of the famous. You've read his biography?

SYDNEY: I've read several.

BROD: Excuse me. There is only one. Mine.

SYDNEY: You've written a biography of Kafka?

BROD: I wrote the biography. I edited the diaries. I published the novels. You want to know about Kafka, start here. Max Brod. (*They shake hands.*)

SYDNEY: Max Brod! You are Max Brod? You're pulling my leg. No. (*Laughs nervously.*) How could you be?

BROD: Why?

SYDNEY: You're Kafka's closest friend.

BROD: Correction. Not his closest friend. His only friend. His only real friend.

SYDNEY: You're a great man. A legend. What would you be doing here? Max Brod!
(*He shakes hands again.*)

BROD: What about Nurse Cavell? Doesn't she want to shake hands with a legend?

LINDA: Brod? You spell it B–R–O–D?
(*She goes to look it up.*)

SYDNEY: No need to look him up. I know all about him.

BROD: (*To audience*) She's about to discover I'm dead. But then I'm also famous. These are the dead ones. Nobody's ever heard of them. That's death. You read my book?

15

SYDNEY: Every word.

LINDA: (*Beckoning him with a book*) Sydney.

SYDNEY: I've read half-a-dozen biographies but I always come back to yours.

BROD: Of course you do. I knew Kafka. They didn't.

LINDA: Sydney, can I have a word?

SYDNEY: In a minute, Linda. Tell me, was Kafka as saintly as you make him out?

(BROD's *interest throughout this conversation is in* LINDA, *not Kafka and still less* SYDNEY.)

BROD: I should lie? Kind, modest and with that clod of a father . . .what type of a nurse was this, crisp, white uniform, thin, black stockings . . . that type?

LINDA: Yes. Strict. And I was a past master of the enema. Sydney.

SYDNEY: (*Eluding* LINDA's *attempts to draw him aside*) To me Kafka is the last, authentic, modern saint. It's interesting that one by one the moral giants of the twentieth century have all been toppled. I say that in my article. 'It is interesting that one by one the moral giants of the twentieth century have all been toppled.' But not Kafka.

BROD: That's fascinating. Nurses have a reputation for unbridled promiscuity. How does that accord with your experience?

LINDA: Sydney.

SYDNEY: Take Wittgenstein. People said he was a saint, but not any more.

LINDA: (*Feigning interest*) No?

SYDNEY: Biography reveals that his less philosophical moments were spent picking up youths.

BROD: What for, when there's so much else on offer?

SYDNEY: And who nowadays admires Freud?

LINDA: Oh? Where did he slip up?

SYDNEY: Dishonest. Freud was quite small . . .

BROD: Minute. He would only have come up to here (*on* LINDA).

SYDNEY: And yet in a photograph of Freud with his colleagues he's head and shoulders above everybody else. Why? Biography reveals he's stood on a box.

LINDA: Oh. Like Alan Ladd.

SYDNEY: Alan Ladd?

LINDA: Alan Ladd wasn't tall. He often had to stand on a box. Either that or his leading lady stood in a trench. Maybe Freud wasn't on a box. Maybe the others were in a trench.

SYDNEY: Linda. Nursing, though an admirable profession, doesn't exactly hone the mind.

BROD: Don't worry about it.

LINDA: But Sydney. You said literary criticism was about unexpected connections. You can't get more unexpected than Freud and Alan Ladd.

BROD: That's the danger with big tits. The mind goes on holiday.

LINDA: Sydney, I want to tell you something.

SYDNEY: Linda, I'm talking. You wouldn't catch Kafka standing on a box. Wanting to make himself bigger. Not your friend Kafka, eh?

BROD: No.

SYDNEY: In fact, I'd have said the reverse. I'd have said he wanted to make himself smaller. Would you agree?

BROD: Larger, smaller, one or the other. You don't still have your uniform?

LINDA: Where's the tortoise gone?
(*She gets down on her hands and knees to look, further fascinating* BROD.)

SYDNEY: We only have to look at his work. Who does Kafka identify with? An ape, a mouse, a cockroach. Smaller and smaller.

BROD: Can I help?

SYDNEY: I tell you, give him a few more years and he'd have needed a microscope to see what he was writing about. I actually say that in my article: 'Give him a few more years and he'd have needed a microscope to see what he was writing about.'

BROD: How interesting. Will it ever stop? If I never hear the name Kafka again it will be too soon.
(*He sits down again, utterly at ease.*)

LINDA: Sydney. You don't think he is this man?

SYDNEY: I'm not sure. Max Brod was a hunchback.

LINDA: Sydney. He's also dead. I looked him up for you. (*Shows him the book.*) Died in 1968.

SYDNEY: In Tel Aviv, yes.

LINDA: You know?

SYDNEY: Of course.

LINDA: So who is he?

SYDNEY: He could be to do with father. A health visitor perhaps.

LINDA: Masquerading as a friend of Kafka?

SYDNEY: The social services are notorious for their imagination.

LINDA: So why not ask him?

SYDNEY: Linda. Don't *worry*. We are having a conversation. Ideas are being exchanged, hypotheses put forward. For me this is a treat. A picnic of the mind. How often do I find someone who's even heard of Kafka let alone someone who can't wait to discuss him?

LINDA: Yes, Sydney.

SYDNEY: All in good time.

LINDA: Yes, Sydney.

(SYDNEY *finds the tortoise.*)

SYDNEY: Here he is. Why don't you put him under the tap?

LINDA: I'll go put him under the tap.

BROD: Can I help?

LINDA: No. You stay and have a picnic with my husband.

(*She exits.*)

SYDNEY: There's one question I must ask you.

BROD: I won't answer it.

SYDNEY: You don't know the question.

BROD: I don't know the question? I don't know the question? There is only one question. Always there has been just one question. 'Why did you not burn the papers?' Nobody, *nobody* is grateful. But for me there would have been no Kafka. He would not have existed. He would have been a no-name. A big zero. I made Kafka. Me! Max Brod. So is it 'Thank you, Max', 'Much obliged, Max', 'Good thinking, Max'? No. Always it's 'Why did you not burn the papers?' Well, there is one person who would thank me. The man himself. If Kafka were around today he'd be the first person to shake my hand.

(There is a shrill scream from LINDA *offstage and* KAFKA *appears on the stage beside* BROD.)*

LINDA: Sydney! Sydney!

BROD: You!

*(*KAFKA *takes his hand as* LINDA *enters.)*

LINDA: It's that tortoise. I'd swilled it under the tap and put it on the draining board. Just then it popped its little head out . . . I don't know what made me do it . . . I gave it a kiss.

BROD: Kafka.

SYDNEY: Kafka? Linda. I believe this is Kafka. It is. It is. Linda. This is Kafka.

LINDA: Sydney.

KAFKA: How are you?

BROD: Good. Terrific. You?

KAFKA: Terrible.

(They laugh.)

BROD: You haven't changed.

KAFKA: *(Embracing him)* Max, Max. Old friend.

SYDNEY: *(Shyly)* How do you do.

KAFKA: *(Taking* LINDA's *hand)* How do you do.

LINDA: *(Panicking)* Sydney.

SYDNEY: Have I the pleasure of addressing Mr Kafka?

*(*KAFKA *nods graciously and diffidently shakes hands.)*

I just don't believe it. Kafka!

KAFKA: Max. Who is this man?

SYDNEY: Linda. It's him. It's Kafka.

LINDA: Sydney. Kafka's dead. They're both dead.

SYDNEY: I know. But it's Kafka.

LINDA: Sydney.

KAFKA: Max. Kindly ask him not to keep saying my name. You remember I never liked my name. The persistent repetition of it is still deeply offensive.

BROD: Sure. I remember. Listen, boys and girls. Kafka doesn't like his name. Point taken. No more Kafka. *(To* KAFKA) The husband's very dull but the wife has possibilities.

SYDNEY: I love you. You're my hero.

KAFKA: Hero? Max, what is this?

LINDA: Excuse me. I hope I'm not out of order but two minutes ago you were a tortoise. Suddenly you're a leading light in European literature.

BROD: My dear Miss Marple. This is someone who wrote a story about a man waking up as a cockroach. So? Now it's a two-way traffic.

LINDA: That was fiction. Wasn't it, Sydney? This is non-fiction.

KAFKA: (*To audience*) What is this about a leading figure in European literature?

SYDNEY: Kafka at 27 Batcliffe Drive!

KAFKA: Max. Is this man deaf? He is still saying my name.

BROD: People. Please. This is the second time of asking. Drop Kafka's name.

(SYDNEY *and* LINDA *draw aside*.)

KAFKA: What is all this 'leading figure in European literature' stuff?

BROD: Well?

KAFKA: I'm nobody. I brought out a few short stories and an unsuccessful novel – that was seventy years ago in Czechoslovakia. How am I a leading figure?

BROD: Did I say modest? Move over E. M. Forster. A saint.

KAFKA: And Max. A beetle.

BROD: Say again.

KAFKA: Not a cockroach. You said cockroach. It was a beetle.

BROD: Will you listen to this man. I make him world famous and he quibbles over entomology.

(BROD *and* KAFKA *draw aside*.)

LINDA: Call the police.

SYDNEY: What for? Nobody's committed a crime.

LINDA: Sydney. It's a Tuesday afternoon. We're expecting someone from the Health Authority and meanwhile you're kicking around some thoughts about Kafka. A knock on the door and it's a stranger with a dripping wet tortoise in his hand, who, lo and behold, turns out to be the world's leading authority on Kafka. Notwithstanding this person seems to have died several years ago you engage him in conversation while I go and swill the tortoise. The next minute it's gone, we've got Kafka in the lounge and these two are falling into one another's arms.

SYDNEY: Well?

LINDA: It just seems a bit too plausible to me.

SYDNEY: So who are they?

LINDA: Burglars.

SYDNEY: Don't be absurd. How many burglars have heard of Franz Kafka?

LINDA: Sydney, they read all sorts in prison. They no sooner get them inside nowadays than they're pestering them to read Proust. That's all some of them go to prison for, the chance of a good read.

SYDNEY: It would have to be a subtle burglar who got in disguised as a tortoise. It's not logical.

LINDA: Criminals have no logic. A woman last week answers the door, the caller shoves a dishcloth in her mouth and steals the television set. You say he couldn't be a tortoise, she's now a vegetable, so don't talk to me about logic. Call the police. Let them decide if he's Kafka.

SYDNEY: What with? Sniffer dogs trained in Modern Studies?

LINDA: Sydney, he's dead. They're both dead.

SYDNEY: They're alive to me. Franz Kafka is more present, more real to me than . . . than . . .

LINDA: I know. Than I am.

SYDNEY: When do we ever talk, Linda?

LINDA: Sydney, we're always talking.

SYDNEY: Not about ideas, Linda. About candlewick bedspreads. The electricity bill. Your mother's eczema. That's what you talk about.

LINDA: I do not. Mother's eczema cleared up last week. I told you, she got some new ointment. And I know I don't talk about candlewick bedspreads because they went out years ago. That's why we should get rid of ours. We want a continental quilt. (*Pause.*) We could afford one. The electric bill's quite reasonable. All right. I'm not clever. Why do you think I want to learn? Only you won't teach me. So I'm boring.

SYDNEY: Linda . .

LINDA: But if it's a choice between boredom and burglary I'm calling the police.

(*She goes off with* SYDNEY *in hot pursuit.*)

KAFKA: I just think it's odd her calling me a leading figure in European literature.

BROD: It is odd. (*Aside*) Wait till I tell him he's world famous, the author of several major masterpieces.

KAFKA: He seemed to think I was somebody too.

BROD: This is England. It doesn't take much to be a celebrity here. (*Aside*) He is going to be over the *moon*.

KAFKA: I published so little and you destroyed the rest.

BROD: (*Aside*) Good job I didn't.

KAFKA: You did, didn't you?

BROD: Of course. It was your last wish.

KAFKA: Dear, faithful Max.

BROD: Though say I hadn't burned it all. And say . . . it's ridiculous of course . . . but say you turned out to be quite famous. You wouldn't mind?

KAFKA: Mind? No. I wouldn't mind. It's just that I'd never forgive you.

BROD: But I'm your best friend.

KAFKA: So it's worse. You'd have betrayed me. No. That would be it between us. Over. Finish. Still, what are we talking about? You burned them. I'm not famous. Everybody's happy.

BROD: Happy? I'm ruined!

(LINDA *returns with* SYDNEY *in hot pursuit.* LINDA *bent on confronting* KAFKA.)

SYDNEY: You know nothing about this.

LINDA: I just want to find out exactly who they are.

SYDNEY: Linda.

LINDA: Can I ask you some questions?

KAFKA: Of course.

SYDNEY: She means about your work.

LINDA: I mean about you.

BROD: His work. She mustn't ask him about his work. Oh, my God.

KAFKA: Feel free. Ask any question you like.

BROD: I'm sorry. Sorry. I don't want any questions. Kafka does not want questions.

22

KAFKA: What about my work?

BROD: What about his work? There is no work. I burnt all the work.

KAFKA: I don't mind talking about my work.

BROD: Exactly. Who are these people anyway? . . . You don't?

KAFKA: Why should I? I worked in an insurance office.

BROD: What am I talking about? Of course you did. Kafka worked in an insurance office. Tell us about it. It sounds fascinating.

LINDA: Sydney works in insurance too.

BROD: Really? How boring.

SYDNEY: I didn't mean that work I meant your real work.

BROD: What is this, some kind of interrogation? (*Recovering himself*) I have to tell you, this is a shy man.

KAFKA: Max, I'm not. He always thought I was shy. I wasn't. I even went to a nudist colony.

LINDA: That is brave.

BROD: Not if you don't take your trunks off.

SYDNEY: Excuse my asking, but why didn't you take your trunks off? Had you something to hide?

KAFKA: Yes. *No.*

SYDNEY: I have this theory that biographies would benefit from a photograph of the subject naked.

KAFKA: Naked? What a terrible idea.

BROD: Shocking. And who, pray, is talking about biography? *No one.* No one at all. In the meantime, old friend, let's recall why you went to that nudist camp in the first place. You were delicate. You had a bad chest, remember. So why don't you just step out into the garden and fill what's left of your lungs with some fresh air.

KAFKA: Max. It is raining.

BROD: Here is an umbrella.

KAFKA: Max!

(*But he goes, bundled out into the garden by* BROD.)

LINDA: I'm calling the police now, while he's in the garden. (*She exits.*)

SYDNEY: (*Ready to go after her*) Why? They can't arrest him. He's committed no crime.

23

BROD: Calm down. He wrote the script for that one. (*Sits down.*)
Cigar?

SYDNEY: I don't smoke.

BROD: Neither do I. Look . . .

SYDNEY: Sydney.

BROD: Syd. There's been a small misunderstanding. Nothing of
importance. You recall how at one point in his life Kafka
intimated I might consider burning his writings?

SYDNEY: On his deathbed, yes.

BROD: (*Furious again*) It was not his deathbed. It was prior to his
deathbed. He was around for years after that. (*To audience*)
Blood and sand, why does everybody round here think
they're an authority on Kafka? He thinks he knows about
Kafka. *Kafka* thinks he knows about Kafka. I'm the only
one who really knows.

SYDNEY: What is he doing in the garden?

BROD: God knows. Giving the kiss of life to an ant, probably.
Why wasn't I a friend of Ernest Hemingway? Where are you
going?

SYDNEY: I've some questions I want to ask him . . .

BROD: No, look . . .

SYDNEY: Sydney.

BROD: OK, Syd. I didn't burn the papers . . .

SYDNEY: (*Trying to go out into the garden again*) That's one of my
questions. Does he mind?

BROD: *Syd.* No! Of course he doesn't mind. Why should he
mind? Still if it's all the same to you I'd rather
you . . . deferred the question a while.

SYDNEY: Why?

BROD: Why? Yes, why? Because . . . because he doesn't know.

SYDNEY: He doesn't know what?

BROD: He doesn't know I didn't burn the papers.

SYDNEY: He doesn't know you didn't burn the papers!

BROD: So what? He is not going to mind.

SYDNEY: No?

BROD: No. Why should he?

SYDNEY: Why should he? That's right. As you say in your book.
This is a saint.

24

BROD: Sure, sure.

SYDNEY: He'll forgive you.

BROD: Nothing to forgive.

SYDNEY: In fact he'll be pleased.

BROD: Pleased? He'll be ecstatic.

SYDNEY: I would be. Can I be the one to tell him? I'd like that.

BROD: No. Not yet.

SYDNEY: When?

BROD: When? Well, I think we've got to be very careful about this. Choose the moment. And while we're on the subject, less of this 'leading figure in European literature' stuff.

SYDNEY: Why?

BROD: Because, dummy, if I had burnt his papers he wouldn't be, would he?

SYDNEY: No, I suppose he wouldn't. What you're saying is he doesn't know he's Kafka.

BROD: He knows he's Kafka. He doesn't know he's *Kafka*.

SYDNEY: Mmm. It's a tricky one.

BROD: Why don't we play a game? He thinks he has no reputation at all. Let's pretend he *has* no reputation at all. Then come the right moment Max here will spill the beans and we can all have a big laugh.

SYDNEY: Yes. A big laugh, yes. Ha ha.

BROD: Where is the bathroom?

SYDNEY: Follow me. Wouldn't that be a lie?

BROD: Listen, Syd. I am Max Brod. I was short-listed for the Nobel Prize. Don't tell me about lies. Here he comes.

SYDNEY: Wait. Let me get this right. The game is: I don't know him, I've never heard of him.

BROD: Right.

SYDNEY: Though when you do get round to telling him, I'd like him to autograph his books.

BROD: Weidenfeld and Nicolson! His books! We've got to get rid of his books.

(BROD *rushes to the bookcase and starts removing books as* KAFKA *comes in.*)

KAFKA: Books?

BROD: Yes. Well, no. You could call them books. They're dirty

25

books. Pornography. Smut.

(SYDNEY *looks hurt, and opens his mouth to protest but thinks better of it.*)

KAFKA: How despicable. His poor wife. I remember I once said 'A book should be like an axe to break up the frozen seas within us.'

(BROD *joins in to finish the quotation.*)

BROD: Well, these are some of the ones that failed the test.

(SYDNEY *is helping to shift the books outside also.* SYDNEY *often has to retrieve books right from under* KAFKA's *nose.*)

KAFKA: Excuse me. I . . . I thought I saw my name.

SYDNEY: Your name? Sorry . . . (*Winking at* BROD) What was your name again?

KAFKA: Kafka. Franz Kafka.

SYDNEY: No, no. This is the Hollywood movie director. Frank Capra.

KAFKA: (*Wistfully, looking at the bookshelves*) It's like looking for one's headstone in a cemetery.

(BROD *is carrying another pile of books out when* SYDNEY *bumps into him and the books go all over the floor.*)

What's that?

SYDNEY: What?

KAFKA: That one. It says *Kafka's Novels*.

SYDNEY: This? *Kafka's Novels*? No. *Tarzan's Navel*.

BROD: (*Quickly taking it*) Anthropology.

KAFKA: And that one. *The Loneliness of Kafka*.

SYDNEY: *The Loneliness of Kafka*? No. *The Loneliness of Raffia*. As an adjunct to her nursing course my wife did occupational therapy. Hence this one: *Raffia: The Debate Continues. The Agony of Raffia*, the endless plaiting, the needle going in and out, suddenly the needle slips, ah! Few people realize the single-minded devotion that goes into the humble table mat.

(*By this time* SYDNEY *thinks he has gathered up all the fallen books. However one has eluded him.* SYDNEY *and* BROD *are transfixed with horror as* KAFKA *picks it up.*)

KAFKA: Proust.

SYDNEY: Great man. A genius.

KAFKA: You think?

26

BROD: Listen. A bit more get up and go and you'd have run rings round him.

KAFKA: I was ill. I had a bad chest.

SYDNEY: Proust had a worse chest than you.

KAFKA: How does he know about my chest?

BROD: He doesn't. (Fool!) Anyway, what is this, the TB Olympics?

KAFKA: (*Reading Proust*) 'For a long time I used to go to bed early.' For a long time I scarcely went to bed at all.

SYDNEY: Yes, only Proust wrote a major novel. What did you do? Sorry, what *is* your name again?

BROD: (*Aside*) Don't overdo it.

SYDNEY: Then *hurry*.

KAFKA: (*To* MAX) Who is this Proust?

SYDNEY: Who is this Proust? *Who is this Proust?* Beg pardon. Only the greatest writer of the twentieth century.

KAFKA: (*Meaning 'protect me against this terrible information'*) Max. (SYDNEY *distracts* KAFKA *while* BROD *runs in and out removing books.*)

SYDNEY: Proust is a lifelong invalid and sufferer from asthma. Lesser men this would stop. *Oui.* Does it stop Proust? *Non.* He lives on a noisy street, the noisiest street in Paris. So, does he sit back and say 'It's too noisy. I can't write here' '*Il y a beaucoup de bruit. Je ne peux pas écrire ici*'? Not at all.

BROD: *Pas du tout.*

SYDNEY: *Eh bien*, what does he do?

BROD: *Qu'est ce qu'il fait*?

SYDNEY: *Le voilà.* He builds himself a cork-lined room . . . *une chambre* (*looking to* BROD *for the translation*) . . .

BROD: (*Lamely*) Cork-lined.

SYDNEY: And in this room . . . (*Showing signs of weariness by now*) *dans cette chambre* . . . *il* . . .

KAFKA: Oh shut up. Max. My room was noisy. It was next door to my parents. When I was trying to write I had to listen to them having sexual intercourse. I'm the one who needed the cork-lined room. And he's the greatest writer of the twentieth century. Oh God.

BROD: Listen. More than Proust ever wrote you burned. Or I burned . . .

(BROD *thinks he has cleared the books when* LINDA *returns with a pile.*)

LINDA: Sydney. These don't belong in the hall.

BROD: Oh my God!

LINDA: What's the matter with the bookcase?

SYDNEY: Full. Chock-a-block.

LINDA: There's tons of room.

KAFKA: (*Helping*) Allow me.

LINDA: Thank you.

SYDNEY: No. (*Seizing the books*) I'm . . . I'm throwing them out.

LINDA: What for?

SYDNEY: (*Nonplussed*) What for?

BROD: He's . . . he's selling them to me.

LINDA: (*Seizing the books back*) The penny drops. I've heard about people like you. Insinuating yourself into people's homes. Sydney. This is how mother lost her gate-legged table.
(*A book falls.* KAFKA *stoops for it, but* BROD *is there first.*)

BROD: Give me that.

LINDA: Look. He can't wait to get his hands on them.

SYDNEY: Linda, (*seizing the books again*) I just want them outside.

LINDA: Why?

SYDNEY: (*Desperately to* BROD) Why?

BROD: I need to go to the toilet. Now.

SYDNEY: Well, for God's sake don't do it over the goldfish or else we'll be entertaining the Brontë sisters.
(*He rushes out after* BROD *carrying the books, leaving* KAFKA *and* LINDA *alone for the first time.*)

KAFKA: You think I'm a criminal?

LINDA: I think your friend is.

KAFKA: Perhaps you should think of me as a dream.

LINDA: I've rung the police.

KAFKA: The police also have dreams.

LINDA: They didn't think you were from the Health Authority.

KAFKA: That's not surprising. I never had much to do with either Health or Authority. The only authority I had came from sickness. TB.

28

LINDA: Sydney had TB. That's how we met. They can cure it now.

KAFKA: I'm sure people find other things to die of.

LINDA: If they take that attitude they probably do.

KAFKA: You sound like a girl I used to know.

(LINDA *sits down and crosses her legs.*)

I say, that's good.

LINDA: What?

KAFKA: The way you took one of your legs and just flung it over the other. You've done it again. Perfect.

LINDA: Don't be silly. Everybody can do that.

KAFKA: No.

LINDA: I just don't think about it.

KAFKA: But in order not to think about it one has to give it a good deal of thought.

(LINDA *tries it again and muffs it.*)

LINDA: It's a simple thing. Like walking.

KAFKA: Is walking simple? Stand up.

(LINDA *stands up.*)

You are going to cross the room. For a start you must decide which leg you're going to move first. Have you come to a decision? Wait. Remember when you're moving whichever leg it is you've decided to move first you should meanwhile be thinking about the one you're going to move after that. Slowly. Oh, you've chosen that leg. I see. Now the other leg. Now the first leg. Now the same leg as you used the time before last. And now this one again, which is the one you used the time before that.

(LINDA *starts to laugh and stagger and pealing with laughter falls into* KAFKA's *arms. At which point* BROD *and* SYDNEY *enter.*)

SYDNEY: Linda.

LINDA: He was just teaching me how to walk.

SYDNEY: Oh. I thought you'd just about got that licked.

BROD: Can I help?

LINDA: Don't touch me.

BROD: It's always the same. As soon as they meet him it's goodnight Max.

LINDA: How slim you are.

KAFKA: I know. Forgive me.

SYDNEY: Odd when one remembers what a big man your father
was.

KAFKA: A giant . . . how did you know that?

SYDNEY: Er, he told me. Didn't you?

BROD: Did I? Of course I did. 'What a big man his father was', I
remember saying. This isn't a game.

SYDNEY: I thought you said it was.

BROD: What about her? She won't give us away.

SYDNEY: No. She's not an intellectual. This is just an ex-nurse.
Say Heidegger to her and she thinks it's a lager.

LINDA: Sydney has a father too.

KAFKA: It's not uncommon.

LINDA: Only he doesn't pick his ears with a toothpick.

KAFKA: My father used to do that.

LINDA: I know.

KAFKA: How?

SYDNEY: I told her.

BROD: And I told him.

KAFKA: You say this Proust is well thought of?

BROD: Not by me. It's a sick mind.

LINDA: He liked boys.

KAFKA: (*Shocked*) Boys?

LINDA: I know. Some men do. Wittgenstein did. Whoever he was

BROD: Not an intellectual? This is Susan Sontag! What does it
matter? Nobody blames them. They're dead. Death does
that for writers. 'Death is to the individual like Saturday
evening is to the chimneysweep: it washes the dirt from his
body.'

KAFKA: That's not bad, Max. I'd like to have said that.

BROD: You did, Kafka, you did. It was one of the things I burnt.

KAFKA: I was better than I thought.

BROD: You were.

KAFKA: What a pity.

SYDNEY: (*Nudging* BROD) Go on. Now.

BROD: There's something I have to tell you.

SYDNEY: I can't wait for this.

LINDA: What?

BROD: It's about burning your books.

SYDNEY: Here it comes.

KAFKA: No need to tell me, old friend. I know.

BROD: You know?

KAFKA: I know.

BROD: (*To* SYDNEY) He knows.

SYDNEY: (*To* LINDA) He knows.

LINDA: Knows what?

BROD: And . . . you don't blame me?

KAFKA: Why should I blame you? How could I?

BROD: Will you listen to this man. Did I say a saint? Shake hands with a saint. He knows.

LINDA: What do you know?

KAFKA: Once upon a time I asked my friend here to destroy all my writings. I know that he feels bad because he obeyed me.

BROD: He doesn't know.

KAFKA: Don't *worry*. I sometimes feel the same. But what's done is done.

BROD: I'm going to have to try a different tack.

SYDNEY: You are.

LINDA: Sydney . . .

SYDNEY: Be quiet.

BROD: Old friend, from that distinguished bundle which I so dutifully thrust into the incinerator I'd like to recall a particularly choice example of what perished that day: 'Somebody must have been telling lies about Joseph K . . .' (KAFKA *joins in*.) '. . . because one fine morning he woke up and found himself under arrest.'

KAFKA: I remember. Two mysterious men arrive to arrest Joseph K who doesn't know what offence he has committed. Then he has to appear before a tribunal somewhere.

BROD: And to get to the courtroom he has to go through somebody's kitchen . . .

LINDA: Really?

(*She glances round her kitchen*.)

KAFKA: . . . where people just seemed to take him for granted. He never does find out what he's done.

BROD: And in the end he's executed.

KAFKA: Did I ever give that one a title?

BROD: A great title: *The Trial* by Franz Kafka.

KAFKA: That doesn't make it sound like a detective story?

SYDNEY: The public like detective stories.

BROD: Only what have we got instead? A short story about a guy who wakes up as a cockroach.

KAFKA: A beetle, Max. A beetle. Why can you never get it right?

BROD: Listen, for all the good you would have done for yourself he could have woken up a fucking centipede.

KAFKA: Max!

LINDA: One more off-colour remark and he'll have to leave, won't he, Sydney? Won't he?

(FATHER *has entered in his overcoat with a little attaché case. He is carrying the orange Penguin book he took in the first scene. He catches Linda's last phrase and assumes it was meant for him.*)

FATHER: Leave? Well, I'm ready. Somebody's been telling lies about me. They've come to take me away and I don't know what I've done.

SYDNEY: Sit down, Father.

LINDA: I'll get him a tablet. Father thinks we're going to put him in a home.

KAFKA: And are you?

LINDA: We didn't want to. But he's driven us so mad asking when, we decided in the end we'd better.

KAFKA: I sympathize. I hated my father. I once wrote him a letter telling him so. Why one can't just get rid of parents I don't understand. One puts the cat out when it's a nuisance, why not them?

SYDNEY: Your father was different.

KAFKA: How do you know?

BROD: How many more times? Because I told him.

(BROD *exits to the garden.* LINDA *exits for a tablet.*)

SYDNEY: Listen, Father. They won't take you away if you can answer some simple questions. The day of the week.

FATHER: Yes. I've got that off by heart.

SYDNEY: The name of the Prime Minister.

FATHER: Yes.

32

SYDNEY: And some simple sums. Hang on to those and you'll be all right.

KAFKA: In youth we take examinations to get into institutions; in old age to keep out of them.

FATHER: (*Putting the Penguin down*) You said this was a detective. It's not a detective at all.

(LINDA *returns with the tablet.*)

LINDA: There are no detectives.

(SYDNEY *assists* LINDA *as she takes* FATHER *out.*)

You have a beautiful Portuguese rug in your room; I can't think why you want to keep coming down here.

(KAFKA *is alone on the stage. He picks up the Penguin and looks at it idly. Then less idly. He reads aloud the first sentence:*)

KAFKA: 'Somebody must have been telling lies about Joseph K because one fine morning he was arrested . . .' (*Turns the book over to look at the title. There is a moment of shocked silence, then he shouts:*) MAX!

(*Nobody comes.* KAFKA *rushes off the stage and comes back with some of the books taken out of the bookshelf, looking at them and throwing them down as he comes.*) Kafka! Kafka! Novels, stories, letters. Everything. MAX!

(BROD *creeps on to the stage.*)

BROD: (*Faintly*) Sorry.

KAFKA: Sorry? SORRY? Max. You publish everything I ever wrote and you're sorry! I trusted you.

BROD: You exaggerated. You always did.

KAFKA: So, I say burn them, what do you think I mean, *warm* them?

BROD: I thought it was just false modesty.

KAFKA: All modesty is false, otherwise it's not modesty. There must be every word here that I've ever written.

LINDA: (*Coming in*) What did he do?

KAFKA: It's not what he did. (*Indicating the books*) It's what he didn't do. *This is* what he did.

(SYDNEY *comes in with a further pile of books.*)

Did I write these too? Oh my God!

SYDNEY: No. These are some of the books about you. Only a few. I believe the Library of Congress catalogue lists some fifteen thousand.

33

KAFKA: Max. What have you done to me?

BROD: Ask not what I've done to you, but what you've done for humanity. You, who never knew you were a great man, now rank with Flaubert, Tolstoy and Dostoevsky, called fellow by the greatest names in literature. As Shakespeare spoke for mankind on the threshold of the modern world you speak mankind's farewell in the authentic voice of the twentieth century.

KAFKA: (*In a small, awe-stricken voice*) Shit.

SYDNEY: He's taking it very badly.

BROD: Don't worry. He'll be all over me in a minute. But who else would treat fame like this, eh? Chekhov? He'd be round at the estate agents, looking at a little place in the country with paddock and mature fruit trees attached. Zola would be installing a Jacuzzi. Even T. S. Eliot'd have people round for drinks. But what does Kafka do?

SYDNEY: Finds the whole thing a trial.

BROD: Exactly. The humility of the man. I tell you, if I were Jesus Christ I'd be looking over my shoulder.

KAFKA: Judas!

SYDNEY: He's made you one of the biggest names in twentieth-century literature.

LINDA: Even I've heard of you.

KAFKA: (*With exaggerated patience*) I didn't want a big name. I wanted a small name. I shrank my name. I pared it down to nothing. I'd have been happy with no name at all.

SYDNEY: But that's the secret of your success. You've got a name for anonymity. *The Trial*: a nameless man's search for justice in a faceless bureaucracy. When Eastern Europe went communist this was the book that told you about it before it happened. In so many words . . .

KAFKA: That's it. That's it. So many words. I've added so many words to the world I've made it heavier.

BROD: Some day you'll thank me.

KAFKA: Max, this is some day.

(BROD *is going to speak*.)

I don't want to speak to you. If you want to talk to somebody talk to Kafka.

SYDNEY: But you are Kafka.

KAFKA: No, I'm not. Kafka is a vast building; a ramshackle institution in every room and department of which, in every corridor, attic and cellar, students and scholars pore over my text and worry over my work. That isn't me. That is Kafka. Communicate with that. Preferably in triplicate.

SYDNEY: This piece I'm writing about you for the *Journal of Insurance Studies* . . .

KAFKA: Don't talk to me about it. He's the expert.

SYDNEY: No, but . . .

KAFKA: Please.

> (*An awkward silence in which* BROD *and* SYDNEY *are at one side of the stage,* KAFKA *and* LINDA *at the other.*)

LINDA: When did you first get the writing bug then?

KAFKA: I'd rather not talk about it.

LINDA: I have to confess, I've never read a word you've written.

KAFKA: Good.

SYDNEY: Wouldn't understand it if she did.

LINDA: I might. How would you know? You never talk to me. I know tons of things about literature.

SYDNEY: Such as?

LINDA: I know about Scott Fitzgerald for a start.

KAFKA: What about Scott Fitzgerald?

LINDA: He had a small p . . . Nothing.

> (*She smiles.* KAFKA *smiles back. She crosses her legs.*)
> Who's a clever girl then? (*Peal of laughter.*)

SYDNEY: He seems to like her.

BROD: You mean she seems to like him. They always did. He has that kind of social ineptitude women mistake for sincerity.

> (*Another peal of laughter.*)

SYDNEY: Linda. You're making a fool of yourself.

LINDA: No, I'm not. He's nice. You said he was nice. He is nice.

BROD: Listen, you can do better than her. That's what fame means. Walk down the street and you'll be mobbed by autograph hunters, girls ready to do anything, anything just for your signature.

KAFKA: But what do I sign? My name. I hate my name. Fame is my name everywhere.

BROD: That's right. Even on T-shirts. Worn by girls. Girls with no morals and degrees in European Literature. Girls who can mix Jane Austen with the latest developments in foreplay.

LINDA: How does he know?

BROD: Because, *sister*, I'm famous too.

KAFKA: You? What for? Not your novels? They were terrible.

SYDNEY: For these. (*Indicates the books.*) As you're famous so is he. His name is synonymous with yours.

KAFKA: How? I'm not even synonymous with my own name.

BROD: The ingratitude!

LINDA: I understand.

SYDNEY: She doesn't.

LINDA: I wish I could make you happy.

KAFKA: There's only one thing that could make me happy. It's the look on my father's face.

LINDA: Pride?

KAFKA: Disgust. 'Look at this lot, Dad. I showed you.'

BROD: You want to be careful. He might turn up.

(KAFKA *is instantly alarmed.*)

KAFKA: How could he?

LINDA: You turned up.

KAFKA: I'm famous. I exist.

SYDNEY: Your father's famous.

KAFKA: My *father*? My father ran a fancy goods store.

SYDNEY: You were a minor civil servant.

KAFKA: My father was a bully. He made my life a misery. I blame him for everything.

BROD: So. Why do you think he's famous?

KAFKA: No. Tell me it's not true. He's buried and forgotten.

(*There is a ring at the bell.*)

No. Max, what do I do? Hide me. Help me.

(LINDA *has answered the door.*)

LINDA: (*Off*) I'd forgotten I'd called you. (*Entering*) Don't be silly. It's not your father at all. It's a policeman.

(*The* POLICEMAN, *a burly figure in a raincoat, is also* KAFKA's *father,* HERMANN K. *He surveys the company without comment, then circles the room to stand behind* KAFKA.)

POLICEMAN/HERMANN K: Hello, my son.

(KAFKA *confronts his* FATHER *as the curtain comes down.*)

36

ACT TWO

KAFKA *is alone on the stage, his novels and all the books about him in a pile in front of him. Nervously, and with many precautions lest he be seen doing so, he takes up one of the books.* LINDA *comes in before he can open it and he hurriedly puts it back.*

LINDA: I've done you a hamburger (*Showing* KAFKA *a plate*).
SYDNEY: (*Coming in right*) He won't want that.
LINDA: Why?
SYDNEY: He doesn't like meat.
KAFKA: How do you know?
SYDNEY: It's a matter of historical record. (*Exits left.*)
LINDA: Try this instead. (*She shows him another plate.*)
KAFKA: What's that?
LINDA: It's something unexpected I do with avocadoes. Tuck in.
    (*Exits right.*)
SYDNEY: (*Entering left.*) I imagine avocadoes must have been
    pretty thin on the ground in turn-of-the-century Prague.
KAFKA: What do they taste like?
SYDNEY: (*Exiting right*) Soap.
    (KAFKA *looks at the plate with intense suspicion and puts it
    down. He starts to sneak another look at one of his books but is
    again interrupted.* FATHER *enters.*)
FATHER: This is him. He's got authority written all over him.
KAFKA: I want to ask you a question.
FATHER: Here it comes.
KAFKA: Have you ever heard of some called Kafka?
FATHER: (*Who has been about to answer, finds himself baffled*)
    Er . . .
KAFKA: It's supposed to be a household name.
FATHER: You don't want the Prime Minister?
KAFKA: He was a Czech novelist. He died in 1924.
FATHER: Six fours are twenty-four.
    (KAFKA *shakes his head.*)
    I know the Prime Minister. I know the date and I can
    manage on the toilet with the bare minimum of assistance
    but if you're supposed to know the name of Czech novelists

everybody's going to end up in a home. I had fifteen men under me.

FATHER *exits.* KAFKA *examines the quiche suspiciously. Smells it. Holds it up to the light. Looks for somewhere to hide it. Behind a cushion? In a vase? Finally, hearing someone coming, he makes a dash for the bookcase and slips it in there.* LINDA *enters with a glass of milk. She spots the empty plate.*

LINDA: I knew you'd enjoy that.

KAFKA: A novel experience. (*He checks the shelf.*) I put it somewhere between Dostoevsky and Henry James.

LINDA: You know how to flatter a girl. Something else? A chocolate perhaps? I have a box of Black Magic I keep for emergencies.

(KAFKA *shakes his head.*)

Your father ate the hamburger.

KAFKA: He would.

LINDA: I was hoping he'd do that trick of rummaging in his ears with a toothpick then using it to pick his teeth.

KAFKA: And did he?

LINDA: No. He has dentures now anyway.

KAFKA: That's an improvement.

LINDA: He thinks so. He passed them round for inspection.

(KAFKA *groans.*)

KAFKA: And he used to lecture me about *my* eating!

LINDA: The cheek. You're twice the man he is. Your constipation is in textbooks. (*Pause.*) You've never had a stab at marriage then?

KAFKA: How could I? I was on such bad terms with my body there was no room for a third party. You should see me in a bathing costume.

LINDA: It could be arranged.

KAFKA: It wasn't that I didn't like women. In fact I frequently got engaged to them. My fiancées tended to regard me as a species of invertebrate. Marriage was going to give me a backbone.

LINDA: Clever, were they?

KAFKA: By and large. The last one, Dora, was very like you.

LINDA: I'm not clever.

KAFKA: But you are. You are a highly accomplished person.

LINDA: Me? What at?

KAFKA: How you enter a room, for instance, as a few moments ago you entered this room, bringing me a glass of milk. In the left hand you carry the milk. In the other hand a napkin and a box of chocolates. With an object in one hand and two objects in the other you have no hand to close the door, but no sooner does this dilemma present itself than you solve it, the right hand bringing the napkin and the box of chocolates over to the left side and tucking them between the upper part of the left arm and the rest of your body, which together cooperate to keep them clasped there, the linen and the chocolates sandwiched between the material of your dress and the arm, which is partly covered in the same material and partly . . . not. The right hand is now free, so you place it on the doorknob and the fingers on that hand clasp the knob and pull it to. Free at last of the door, you take three steps into the room, one leg effortlessly passing the other (your dress seems to consist of some light, woven fabric) until both legs come to a tentative halt at a point which (even with all these things on your mind, the milk, the chocolates, the moving legs) you have yet managed to find time to select as appropriate. Standing gently at rather than on this spot, you lift the glass of milk towards me, managing as you do so to combine it with fetching the right hand over to the left side to take the napkin and the chocolates, now released by an agreement between your arm and your body. The two hands, one with milk, the other with the napkin and the chocolates, are now brought gently up towards me. I take the napkin and the milk but not the chocolates. To console the chocolates for this rebuff, your left hand steals comfortingly into the box, selects one and carries it to your mouth. Finally, and still holding the chocolates, you sit down.

LINDA: I'm not surprised. I must have been exhausted. You forgot something.

KAFKA: Yes?

LINDA: When I was handing you the glass one of my fingers touched one of yours.

KAFKA: I hadn't forgotten. It was this finger. (*He holds up a finger.*)

LINDA: And this.

(*She holds up her finger. It almost looks as if they might kiss, but they don't as* LINDA *breaks away.* BROD *and* SYDNEY *have entered.*)

SYDNEY: Was it always like this?

BROD: No. I have to tell you. His girlfriends were women of great poise and intelligence or nubile young creatures of seventeen. In either category your wife hardly hits the bull's-eye.

SYDNEY: This is intolerable. Linda.

LINDA: Excuse me. Sydney?

SYDNEY: He should talk to his father.

LINDA: I don't believe he wants to, do you?

KAFKA: No.

LINDA: No.

SYDNEY: Don't listen to her. She doesn't understand you. I've read your books. I admire you. I am a *fan*.

KAFKA: (*To* SYDNEY) You say you know me. I don't want to be known. (*To* LINDA.) He says he understands me: if he did understand me, he'd understand that I don't want to be understood.

LINDA: Of course. I understand that. (*She doesn't.*)

SYDNEY: I read his books and this is the thanks I get.

BROD: It's more thanks than I get and I practically wrote them.

SYDNEY: I've had enough. I'm going to break this up. (SYDNEY *exits, calling as he goes.*) Mr Kafka.

(KAFKA *is instantly alarmed.*)

KAFKA: Help me.

LINDA: I'm going to make a silly suggestion. Why don't you and your father just shake hands?

KAFKA: I can't.

LINDA: Why?

KAFKA: My hand is shaking.

LINDA: You're a grown man.

KAFKA: Not with my father around I'm not.

(HERMANN K *enters, followed by* SYDNEY.)

HERMANN K: Funny. They said I had a son here. They get into the dumbest places, sons. Some even get to the top of the tree. Only a good father tracks them down and brings them back to earth. I'm waiting.

LINDA: What for?

HERMANN K: I'm waiting for this son to fling his arms around me in heartfelt welcome, sink to his knees in abject remorse. I'm waiting for the brittle body and the hot consumptive breath. I'm braced for a kiss.

(KAFKA *doesn't move, frozen in terror.*)

Still as thin as a tram ticket. Did he eat?

(*Many of Hermann K's remarks are addressed to the audience. It's important that he should be on good terms with the audience, have a relationship with them, or he will just seem a bore and a bully. Perhaps it is that only the dead people can talk to the audience and are conscious of them, though* FATHER *talks to the audience too.*)

LINDA: Every scrap.

HERMANN K: He didn't put it down the toilet?

LINDA: No.

HERMANN K: That was his usual trick. Shepherd's pie floating in the toilet: show me a quicker way to break a mother's heart. So where? (*He looks round the room. Behind cushions, under the sofa, etc.*) My son had a problem with food. He didn't like it.

KAFKA: I ate nuts, raisins. Salad.

LINDA: Very healthy.

HERMANN K: For squirrels. I'm told he's done pretty well.

SYDNEY: An understatement.

BROD: No thanks to his father.

HERMANN K: I could debate that with you, Professor. My son is a near-delinquent. A spent condom.

LINDA: You've no business talking like that. This is a sensitive man.

HERMANN K: Lady, I'm the sensitive man. My son is about as sensitive as a gannet.

SYDNEY: You're proud of him. You must be.

HERMANN K: Why? What's he done? Written a book or two. My father could lift a . . .

41

HERMANN K and BROD: (*Together*) . . . sack of potatoes in his
    teeth.
BROD: He won't have read a word he's written.
HERMANN K: I tried to read one once. Flat as piss on a plate.
    When he makes *Reader's Digest*, then I'll read him.
BROD: *Reader's Digest*! Last week I had a telegram from the
    Oxford English Dictionary. Your son is so famous that they
    named a word after him.
HERMANN K: What kind of word?
BROD: An adjective. Kafka-esque.
HERMANN K: I never heard it. Has it caught on?
BROD: Caught *on*? Your son now has adjectival status in Japanese.
KAFKA: Is this true?
SYDNEY: Don't ask her, ask *me*. Of course it's true.
BROD: They don't only write about you. They have to use you to
    write. Now you're a tool of the trade.
KAFKA: Thanks for nothing, Max.
SYDNEY: Of course you're not the only one.
KAFKA: Not Proust again?
SYDNEY: Afraid so. Proustian.
BROD: Kafka-esque is better.
LINDA: Look on the bright side. Most people have never heard of
    either of you.
HERMANN K: How's this word going?
SYDNEY: Famously. It crops up all the time. (*He picks up a
    newspaper*.) Here we are. It's an article about Yves
    St Laurent.
KAFKA: Who's he?
LINDA: A dress designer.
KAFKA: A dress designer?
SYDNEY: 'He is adept at coping with the Kafka-esque intrigues of
    high fashion.'
KAFKA: High fashion? What's this high fashion? I never had
    anything to do with high fashion. What has Kafka to do with
    high fashion?
BROD: Words don't always get used correctly. What matters is
    that they get used.
HERMANN K: Do we get a percentage?

BROD: Words are free.

HERMANN K: If you make people a present of them, sure they are. My son has rights here. I told him this was a no-good friend. His name exploited all over the world and what does he get for it? Can you believe it? Nothing. Well, you'd better get on the phone and stop them.

BROD: How?

HERMANN K: The law. The authorities. Don't they have some control over words?

BROD: Not officially.

KAFKA: I don't understand it. 'Kafka-esque intrigues of high fashion.' I work in an insurance office. I have maybe three or four suits the whole of my life. I die a failure at the age of forty-one. I get into the dictionary and suddenly I'm . . .

SYDNEY: Hardy Amies.

HERMANN K: He should have listened to his father. Incidentally, does my son get to meet any of the models?
(BROD *turns away in despair.*)
Some friend. He gives his name to a word and he can't even get a fuck out of it.

LINDA: (*To* KAFKA) We didn't hear that, did we?

SYDNEY: I'm sure your new friend has heard it before. He may even know what it means.

HERMANN K: I wouldn't bank on it. What would I have done with his chances. (*At the bookcase.*) Edith Sitwell. He could have her. Evelyn Waugh. *Vile Bodies*. She sounds as if she knows how to please a man. I'm still waiting for this kiss.

BROD: His name's an adjective in Japanese. Why should he kiss you?

HERMANN K: I was a simple man. I came from nothing. What was so wrong with my footsteps he didn't want to follow in them?

KAFKA: He sold *buttons*.

HERMANN K: Buttons, would you tell my son with the sick mind, that put him through college. I can see through him. You don't have to go to university to see through your own son . . . So, he wound up a writer. Did I stand in his way? Go, I said. Go. Walk in the high places of the earth. Be rich. Be

43

famous. Only one day come home and lay a single flower on your father's grave.

KAFKA: I died before he did.

HERMANN K: He did. On purpose.

BROD: I was at the funeral. You weren't upset. He wasn't upset at all.

KAFKA: That's right.

HERMANN K: How does he know? He was dead. He was where he always wanted to be, safely tucked up in his grave. He makes me sick standing there.

LINDA: And you make me sick, turning up and laying down the law. You . . . you great bladder of Czechoslovakian lard.

SYDNEY: Linda.

LINDA: Why don't you and I go next door.

KAFKA: Yes.

LINDA: Then I can fix you something more to eat.

KAFKA: Maybe not.

BROD: Old friend. Come with me into the garden.

KAFKA: Yes.

BROD: Then I can tell you how big you are in New Zealand.

KAFKA: I don't want that either.

HERMANN K: Why don't you just talk to your father?

KAFKA: I want that least of all. Oh God!

(*Cornered, he finally makes a bolt for it into the kitchen.* LINDA *smiles happily, and is about to follow him.*)

LINDA: Incidentally, what was the woman's role in this household? What was his mother doing?

BROD: Backing up his father.

HERMANN K: Naturally. We were a normal family.

(LINDA *exits left.* BROD *goes into the garden.* SYDNEY *and* HERMANN K *are alone.*)

So. You're a big fan of my son.

SYDNEY: I'm writing an article about him if that's what you mean. I'm a fool. I thought he'd be interested.

HERMANN K: I'm not interested either. These books, articles . . . they're all the same. For him whitewash, for me excrement.

SYDNEY: Mine would have been different.

HERMANN K: Yes?

44

SYDNEY: Having met your son, I begin to think the books are all mistaken.

HERMANN K: That's interesting. In what way?

SYDNEY: He's not quite the person I imagined him to be. I thought he was a saint.

HERMANN K: You mean you don't any more?

SYDNEY: No. I think posterity's got him wrong. He has faults like everybody else.

HERMANN K: Ladies and gentlemen, I have lain in my grave and dreamed of this moment! Look . . .

SYDNEY: Sydney.

HERMANN K: Syd. I'm not an intellectual. I sold knicker elastic, so you'll forgive me if I spell it out.

SYDNEY: Do. I'm still trying to spell it out myself.

HERMANN K: Misjudge him, they misjudge me. If my son wasn't so good as all the books make him out to be, and I wasn't so bad . . . if we were, say, more just a routine father and son, then I wouldn't be the villain any more and . . .

SYDNEY: And all the books would have to be rewritten.

HERMANN K: And then people would see I was just an ordinary fellow and you'd be famous.

SYDNEY: *I'd* be famous? How?

HERMANN K: A new view of Kafka, of course you would.

SYDNEY: I hadn't thought of that. I could take time off from insurance.

HERMANN K: Time off? Time off? Fifty years of Kafka studies turned on their heads. You could travel the world, lecturing, giving talks . . .

SYDNEY: People would know my name, students. I'd be a personality! (*Pause.*) But only if I'm right. Only if Kafka isn't a saint and you are just an ordinary father and son.

HERMANN K: You *are* right. And I'll prove it. Go fetch the little scallywag.

(SYDNEY *goes off, leaving* HERMANN K *alone.* FATHER *enters, with his walking frame, hat and coat on.*)

FATHER: Do you know what the latest is? Besides the date and the name of the Prime Minister, they ask you the name of a leading Czech novelist.

HERMANN K: Else what?

FATHER: They take you away.

HERMANN K: You can't be expected to know that.

FATHER: Of course I know it. Franz Kafka.

HERMANN K: My son's even more famous than I thought! What about his father?

FATHER: You're not supposed to know about his father?

HERMANN K: Of course. Everybody knows about Kafka's father.

FATHER: Kafka wrote books.

HERMANN K: A book is a coffin and in it is your father's body.

FATHER: I'd better go and swot it up. The buggers. Every time you're ready for the examination they change the syllabus! (*Exits.*)

HERMANN K: Now. This is my chance to come over as a Normal Parent.

(*He opens his arms, rehearsing his first embrace for his son as* LINDA *comes in, pursuing* KAFKA *with food, followed by* SYDNEY.)

LINDA: You'll love it. It's kiwi fruit and satsuma segments. Did they have kiwi fruit in Prague?

KAFKA: No. Thank God.

LINDA: How did they manage?

(HERMANN K *is waiting for* KAFKA, *arms outstretched.*)

HERMANN K: Look at him. Don't you just love him. Come, give your Dad a kiss.

KAFKA: Who? Me? What is this?

HERMANN K: Baby. You've been rumbled.

KAFKA: Rumbled? Don't touch me. What do you mean?

HERMANN K: What do I mean? I love the boy. Forget his faults, I love him.

KAFKA: Dad.

LINDA: It seems the affection is not returned.

HERMANN K: I know. I *know*. Lady, you are so right. That's what it seems. But, as your clever little hubby has found out, things aren't always what they seem. Until this moment everybody thought I hated my son. They thought he hated me. (*He bursts out laughing.*) The truth is, we're devoted to each other.

46

(*He embraces the shrinking* KAFKA.)

Love me, you pillock. Do as I tell you.

LINDA: Leave him alone. Just because you're his father doesn't
mean you can kiss him. He hates his loved ones, we all know
that. You don't believe this?

SYDNEY: Why not?

LINDA: You're pathetic.

SYDNEY: All the evidence about Kafka's father comes from
Kafka. The only son who ever told the truth about his father
was Jesus Christ – and there are doubts about him.

LINDA: But this is a mean, cheap person. Can't you *see*? He's a
fraud.

HERMANN K: (*Kissing* KAFKA) Is this a fraud? Or this?

KAFKA: Father. You hate me, then all of a sudden you love me.
What did I do?

HERMANN K: Listen, you teetering column of urine, this clown is
writing an article about you.

KAFKA: I know.

HERMANN K: So. Don't you see? It's our big chance. We can
be nice people. I love this kid, this is someone really
special.

KAFKA: Our big chance? Your big chance. I am nice people
already.

HERMANN K: Yes. Thanks to me. Thanks to me being the shit.
Bless him.

SYDNEY: Look at that. Do you know what this is, Linda? That is
a breakthrough in Kafka studies.

LINDA: It looks more like somebody getting their arm twisted to
me.

SYDNEY: You used to be proud of me, Linda. You used to trust
me.

LINDA: Sydney. I've talked to him.

SYDNEY: I know. He's scarcely talked to anyone else. I've never
had a look in. I love him.

HERMANN K: So do I.

KAFKA: I don't want to have this conversation.

LINDA: You told me you couldn't stand one another. You blamed
him for everything.

47

HERMANN K: Lying.

LINDA: No.

HERMANN K: Tell her. Tell her it was all your fault. Or else.

KAFKA: Else what?

HERMANN K: Or else, you two-faced pisspot, I tell the world the one fact biographers never know. I reveal the one statistic every man knows about himself but which no book ever reveals. You see, sir, it's as I say, we're just a normal father and son. My normal. (*He indicates about eight inches.*) Your normal. (*He indicates about three inches.*)

KAFKA: No, Dad. You wouldn't.

HERMANN K: No? There is one fact about my son and his . . . old man that has never got into print . . .

LINDA: Stand up to him. Come on.

HERMANN K: The long and the short of the matter is . . .
     (BROD *enters.*)

KAFKA: I was a terrible son. A dreadful son. A real father and mother of a son. And yet my father loved me.

BROD: I don't believe what I'm hearing.

HERMANN K: Here's the real culprit. The original biographer. The man who led posterity up the garden path in the first place.

KAFKA: Max. Help me.

BROD: Suddenly I'm forgiven. So what's the problem?

HERMANN K: You're at it again. The same old game. Coming between a father and a son. Well, not any more. Now for the first time the truth is going on record. Say it again, my son.

KAFKA: My father loved me. It was all my fault.

BROD: Brilliant. And your lips didn't even move. What's he got on you this time?

KAFKA: Nothing. Honestly.

BROD: Listen. Max is back. We're friends again. The old team. Tell this gorilla to get lost.

KAFKA: No, Max.

BROD: Are you saying you lied to me?

KAFKA: Yes.

LINDA: And you lied to me?

KAFKA: I lied to everybody.

48

BROD: Why?

SYDNEY: Because he was a writer. Writers do lie. They exaggerate because they always think they're the injured party. That's one of the things you learn in insurance: the injured party always exaggerates.

HERMANN K: Yes. You boys of art, you're all the same. I want to hear it again. How much did I love you? (*Indicating three inches.*) A little. (*Indicating eight inches.*) Or a lot.

KAFKA: I can't tell you how much.

BROD: I'm nauseated.

LINDA: You're hiding something?

KAFKA: No. It's just that there were faults on both sides.

HERMANN K: We sparred a little, sure, but who doesn't?

BROD: Sparred? 'Eat your meat or I'll get a long spoon and cram it down your throat like they do in prisons.'

HERMANN K: That's me. And you say I was wrong. Dr Spock says I was wrong. The *Cambridge History of Literature* says I was wrong. Does he say I was wrong?

KAFKA: You were right, Father. Parents love their children so they make them eat.

HERMANN K: True?

LINDA: I don't know. We have no children.

HERMANN K: So what do you know about anything?

BROD: You tried to stop him writing. You even hid his ink.

HERMANN K: What time was it?

KAFKA: Three in the morning.

HERMANN K: What time did you have to go to work?

KAFKA: Seven. You were right. A boy needs sleep.

BROD: He tried to stop you writing altogether.

HERMANN K: Of course I did. That's how clever I was. If I'd said 'Stick to the writing', he would probably have ended up a chartered accountant. Hermann Kafka didn't fall off the Christmas tree yesterday. Right, my son?

(KAFKA *nods unhappily.*)

Kiss? Mmmm. Yours a little kiss. Mine a big kiss.

LINDA: I think you might have told me. I told you about Sydney.

SYDNEY: What?

BROD: I'm the one he should have told. I wrote his biography. I gave him to the world. I'm nauseated.

SYDNEY: What about me?

LINDA: I told him I wasn't very happy.

SYDNEY: That's you. You said you'd told him about me.

KAFKA: How long do I have to keep up this charade?

HERMANN K: Until people start liking me more than they like you. Until they realize what a handful you were. Until I get into the books in a proper light and posterity has finally got to hand it to me, that's how long.

KAFKA: It will never happen.

HERMANN K: So should I tell them your little secret . . .?

KAFKA: No!

HERMANN K: Then cuddle me, you soiled bandage. Snuggle up.

KAFKA: *Cuddle* you. I'm Kafka. I never cuddled anyone in my life.

HERMANN K: So you've just made a breakthrough. And not gingerly. If there's one thing I can't stand it's gingerly cuddling. Hey, just look at this boy. Someone take a picture.

BROD: I am nauseated by this. Sick to my scrotum. The shrinking hypocrisy of it. Seen here embracing his son, one of the most notorious shits in literary history.

HERMANN K: (*Gleefully*) I *know*.

BROD: What is it you're hiding?

KAFKA: *Nothing*, honestly.

HERMANN K: Go into the garden, son. Get some fresh air. But remember, I love you.

(BROD *is about to follow.*)

No. Sorry. I think my son would prefer to be alone, wouldn't you son?

KAFKA: Yes, father. (*Exits.*)

BROD: You make me sick.

HERMANN K: I know.

(BROD *exits.*)

So I'm going to come well out of this article?

SYDNEY: An ordinary fellow.

HERMANN K: Well, don't think I'm not grateful. Anything you want in the soft-furnishing line, high-quality fancy goods, you only have to ask. Curtaining materials, rufflette, those little mats you put under glasses to stop them making a nasty ring on a nice polished table . . . A man wants to show his gratitude, exonerated after all these years. I feel sorry for my son, naturally, pushed off his pedestal, but the truth had to come out.

SYDNEY: You were found guilty on false evidence.

HERMANN K: I was. Trial? I never had a trial. This is the joke: my son writes a book about someone who's had up for a crime he didn't commit and everybody thinks the book's about him. It's not. It's about me. In fact, if I weren't so fond of my son I'd say he's the one who should be put on trial.

LINDA: In what way?

HERMANN K: No, no. Forget I said it. Fundamentally this is a good boy.

LINDA: Try him for what?

HERMANN K: Perjury. Bearing false witness against his father.

SYDNEY: It isn't only that. There are other charges. Other questions.

LINDA: But you admired him.

SYDNEY: I did. I do . . . though he's not the man I thought he was. Still, there's no question of you trying him: you're his father.

HERMANN K: You're in insurance. Investigation and assessment, it's right up your street.

LINDA: There's a difference between a man's reputation and a scratch on the bodywork. Sydney's no judge. He's . . .

SYDNEY: What?

LINDA: He's nobody.

SYDNEY: I married you.

LINDA: That proves it, probably.

SYDNEY: Well, I may be a nobody, Linda, but what I am is a reader. And writers are tried by readers every time they open their books. Fetch him. He trusts you. (SYDNEY *places the walking frame to act as a makeshift dock, draws the curtains, and as the stage darkens* BROD *comes on.*)

LINDA: Sydney. This is persecution.

SYDNEY: No, it's not. It's biography.

BROD: My biography never put him in the dock.

SYDNEY: I know. That's what was wrong with it.

(LINDA *goes to fetch* KAFKA. *After a moment* KAFKA *creeps in. He sees the dock waiting.*)

KAFKA: Max, Father . . .

HERMANN K: Don't look at me.

KAFKA: What have I done?

SYDNEY: (*Taking the frame and putting it in front of* KAFKA) You are famous. Fame is a continuing offence. It leaves you open to trial at any time.

KAFKA: But I didn't want fame.

BROD: I know. It's all my fault. But I bet you still expect me to defend you.

LINDA: Why don't I defend you?

SYDNEY: You?

KAFKA: How? You know nothing about me.

LINDA: I like you. Nobody else seems to.

SYDNEY: I do, given the chance.

LINDA: Then why the trial?

SYDNEY: I just want to cut him down to size. If I do that I might make my name. Don't you want me to make my name?

LINDA: No. Not at the expense of his.

SYDNEY: Do you, Sydney, take this bottle of hydrochloric acid, Linda, to be your lawful wedded wife? Splendid. Would you, Linda, take your stiletto heel and force it up the groom's nose? Excellent. I now pronounce you man and wife. *All right*. You defend, I prosecute, and we'll see who wins. Right?

LINDA: Right.

KAFKA: (*In the middle*) Oh dear.

SYDNEY: Very well. Let's kick off with this question of your name. While every other writer one can think of wants to make his name, you want to unmake yours. So you unravel your name until there's only one letter left: K. You sign your letters K, you refer to yourself as K. What was it you disliked about Kafka?

LINDA: What is it you dislike about Sydney?

SYDNEY: I dislike Sydney because it carries within it the

unhatched threat of Syd. And if you can't do any better than that I'd leave it to him (*He indicates Brod*). What was it you disliked about Kafka?

KAFKA: It means jackdaw. A thief. It also means me.

SYDNEY: Can I suggest another reason? The name Kafka. Treat it like an equation in algebra. Take the F to one side of the question and what are we left with? F equals Kaka. Franz is shit. Is that why you disliked it?

LINDA: Better than Syd.

BROD: And T. S. Eliot is an anagram of toilets so does that make him a closet? This isn't biography. It's not even literary criticism. It's the only thing the English are good at . . . . crossword puzzles. He denies it. He denies everything.

KAFKA: F equals Kaka. Truthfully it hadn't occurred to me, but now you point it out it's not a bad idea.

BROD: What do you do with this man?

KAFKA: My name, it was like a tin tied to the tail of a cat. I wanted rid of it.

SYDNEY: Quite, and though you get the credit for trying to lose your name, you never do lose it. You make it famous. And the person who does lose his name gets no credit for it at all.

HERMANN K: Who was that?

SYDNEY: You.

HERMANN K: Me?

SYDNEY: Yes.

BROD: Him?

HERMANN K: That's right. In Prague in 1919 stop any passing housewife and say Kafka and she'd direct you to my shop by the town hall. If it's knicknacks you're after, the name is Kafka!

SYDNEY: And what happens if you say you're Kafka now?

HERMANN K: 'You Kafka?' people say. 'Kafka didn't have a moustache for a start. Kafka is the skinny guy with the big ears on the back of the Penguins.' Suddenly I don't exist. So, Mr Name-Dropper I'm the one who loses his name. Gets de-nominated. Mr Hermann Kafka. Only I didn't lose it. It was taken. By my son.

BROD: All sons take their father's name.

53

LINDA: Not only sons. You took my name. When I married you.

SYDNEY: And?

LINDA: Why is it when a woman gets married we say she takes her husband's name? What we mean is he takes hers. Takes it and buries it.

HERMANN K: All right, so you lose your name too, dear. The point the gentleman is making, precious, is that the one person who didn't lose his name is the person who claimed to want to lose it, and the person who got the credit for losing it: my son.

LINDA: And whose fault is that? (*She points at Brod.*)

BROD: He was in two minds. He was always in two minds. I did him a good turn.

SYDNEY: I've never understood that.

BROD: It's called friendship.

SYDNEY: Did he ever do you a good turn?

KAFKA: I made him famous.

SYDNEY: But that's not a good turn, is it? When Kafka was alive, of the two of you who is the better known?

BROD: I'd published several novels. He'd published almost nothing. I was a poet, a critic. Me, no question. With a comparable reputation in Czechoslovakia I'd probably be in the government.

SYDNEY: And what was Kafka when you knew him?

BROD: A friend of Max Brod.

SYDNEY: Whereas today . . .

BROD: I'm the friend of Kafka.

LINDA: That's nothing to be ashamed of. The great man's friend. That's all a woman gets. That's all a wife would have got.

BROD: But I wasn't his wife. I was someone in my own right.

KAFKA: And my best friend. Rather nice I should have thought.

BROD: If not to exist is nice. And since you do think not existing is nice, maybe it is.

KAFKA: Don't you exist?

BROD: Not any more. I go on publishing novels after you die, notching up steady sales. Only then I start publishing yours. Result: as soon as they read yours they don't want to know about mine. (*He takes out some clippings.*) This is my last novel. It was about the Arab–Israeli War. This reviewer found in it 'a trace of Kafka's imagery but' (here it comes) 'none of that simple fascinating prose style that makes Kafka readable'. You readable! You may have been a genius, but you were never readable. You finished me as a novelist. All I could do was go round lecturing about the Kafka I knew. 'Kafka as I remembered him'. Or Kafka as I remembered remembering him. What you were actually like I'd forgotten till now. I had no life of my own any more.

LINDA: You *were* his wife.

BROD: No, I was his widow.

LINDA: Even better.

SYDNEY: Would you say your friend was good-looking?

BROD: Yes. Yes, I would.

KAFKA: No.

HERMANN K: There has to be something about him, hasn't there? He's my son.

SYDNEY: You think he's good-looking, don't you?

LINDA: In comparison w— Yes.

KAFKA: My body wasn't satisfactory. I couldn't bear to look at it.

SYDNEY: Your diaries show you looked at it all the time.

KAFKA: Only in disgust.

SYDNEY: Do you grumble about your physique to your friend here?

BROD: Does he ever?

KAFKA: Do I? I don't remember.

BROD: When don't you? Every imperfection of the body tormented you. Constipation, a toe that wasn't properly formed, even dandruff. Toes and dandruff. I wished I'd had your problems.

KAFKA: Why?

BROD: Why? You prick in a bottle. You turd in a hat. *Why?* Did you never look at me? My spine was twisted. You're complaining to me about dandruff. I was a *hunchback*.

LINDA: He's not a hunchback now.

BROD: There's not much to be said for death, but it is the end of disability.

SYDNEY: Your sensitive friend.

LINDA: Say something. Defend yourself.

KAFKA: What for? Nobody can reproach me with failings for which I have not reproached myself. List my shortcomings now, I listed them half a century ago. Find fault with me now, what is the evidence: my own fault-finding then. I stand here self-examined, self-confessed and self-convicted.

HERMANN K: Self, self, self.

KAFKA: Nobody ever believed what I said about myself. When I said I exaggerated they thought I was exaggerating. When I said I lied, they thought I lied. I said I was an agent of the devil, they thought this meant I was a servant of God. When I said they must not believe me, they did not believe me. But now you believe me. Only now when at last you find I was telling the truth about myself you call me a liar.

LINDA: I don't think you're a liar.

KAFKA: But you'd agree I was a terrible human being?

LINDA: No. Pretty average, if you ask me.

BROD: Average? Kafka is average?

SYDNEY: And now as in some Czech village wooing Kafka pauses with his rucksack at the garden gate, asks for a lemonade and our brisk Shavian heroine reads him a lesson on life and generally pulling his socks up.

LINDA: When I first saw you I thought here's somebody different. I can talk to this man. And what's more peculiar, he listens. He notices. I also thought what nice hands.

KAFKA: And now?

LINDA: I still like your hands.

KAFKA: But I'm a terrible human being.

LINDA: No.

KAFKA: No?

LINDA: No. You're a man, that's all.

SYDNEY: Oh no.

(*All the men except* KAFKA *groan*.)

KAFKA: Not much of a man.

LINDA: Every inch.

(HERMANN K *sniggers*.)

KAFKA: Dad.

LINDA: You're a man, because, although you despair, at the same

56

time like all men you believe your despair is important. You think you're insignificant but your insignificance is not insignificant. Oh no.

KAFKA: That's because I'm a writer.

LINDA: No. It's because you are a man. Whatever happens or doesn't happen to you matters. You may not want the world to think you're somebody, provided it recognizes you are nobody.

KAFKA: But I am nobody.

LINDA: Why *tell* us? Women can be nobodies all the time and who cares? All these letters to your girlfriends . . . Letters to Milena, letters to Felice. Saved. Published. Where are their letters to you? Lost. Thrown away. That's a man.

KAFKA: I was born a man.

LINDA: What excuse is that? You changed into a beetle, a dog, an ape, the one thing you never transformed yourself into was the lowliest creature of all . . . a woman.

SYDNEY: Good try, but you're wrong. One of the last stories he wrote is about a female, Josephina, a singing mouse.

KAFKA: You're defending me now.

BROD: Against her? Of course he is. We have to stick together. Anyway, why save your girlfriends' letters? Are they literature?

HERMANN K: Women.

LINDA: Are you disappointed in me?

KAFKA: No. I always expect to be disappointed. If I'm not disappointed, then I'm disappointed.

LINDA: I always feel I want to mother him.

KAFKA: No. Once was enough. (KAFKA *tries to leave the dock*.)

SYDNEY: One last point. You never saw fascism, communism, the totalitarian state.

KAFKA: No. By that time I was safely tucked up in my grave.

SYDNEY: Your work suggests you would not have been happy under such regimes.

KAFKA: Does it? I can't say.

SYDNEY: Oh, I think so. Your reputation today, at least among those who know your name but haven't read you (which is the measure of literary reputation after all) . . . your reputation stands high as a man who protested (though don't ask in what respect precisely), a man who shook his fist (helplessly, no doubt) against authority, officialdom, the law. You were, if not an enemy of the state, a friend of the enemies of the state. Is that reputation justified, do you think?

KAFKA: I have told you. Any reputation is a burden. Where would you be happiest?

KAFKA: It's not a place that exists in the world.

SYDNEY: Why?

KAFKA: It would be a place where I am read only by vermin, the outcasts of the community, the convicts and exiles. I would be read by untouchables, furnacemen, sweepers of roads. Furtively, with discretion and behind locked doors. It would be a place where I am read, but not named, known but not spoken of, studied but not taught. That would be my ideal state.

SYDNEY: There was a place like that.

KAFKA: Where? It must be wonderful. I'd like to have lived there.

SYDNEY: You did. It was called Prague. (*He takes the frame away, and puts it offstage.*)

KAFKA: Is the trial over?

SYDNEY: For the time being. (*He takes his manuscript.*) The process goes on, of course, I've no need to tell you that. Articles, books . . . every day is –

KAFKA: – a day of judgement. I know.

(*All clear, leaving* HERMANN K *alone on the stage as* FATHER *comes in, either with his frame or a makeshift version of it, like a chair.*)

FATHER: Don't go. I want you to test me. Ask me any question you want about this Czech novelist *or* his father. I think you'll find it's all at my fingertips.

HERMANN K: What was his father like?

FATHER: Dreadful. And a shocking bully. Made his son's life a misery. The root of all the trouble. Is that right? It is. Ten out of ten. Father goes to the top of the class. Now at last I can reveal the name of the Prime Minister . . .

HERMANN K: Sorry.

FATHER: What?

HERMANN K: You're wrong.

FATHER: I never am. I looked in all the books.

HERMANN K: The books are wrong. Kafka's father was a normal parent.

FATHER: A normal parent? How am I expected to remember a normal parent? I'm a normal parent. Nobody remembers me.

HERMANN K: He was an average father.

FATHER: But the world's full of average fathers. Average fathers are two a penny. An average father? I'm never going to remember that.

(FATHER *goes off leaving* HERMANN K *pensive*.)

HERMANN K: Hermann Kafka, you want your head examining. You're trying to come over as a nice parent and get into all the books. What for? Nice parents don't get into the books. With nice parents there are no books. Damn, damn, damn!

(KAFKA *enters*.)

Listen, son. A change of plan. I want you to do as I tell you.

KAFKA: Haven't you finished torturing me? You've destroyed my character, lost me my best friend . . .

HERMANN K: And now I'm going to do you a good turn.

KAFKA: No, please. Not that. Not a good turn.

HERMANN K: Can I have your attention please? That's everybody.

(FATHER *returns to the stage*.)

No, not you.

FATHER: You said everybody.

HERMANN K: I mean everybody who matters.

(FATHER *exits again as* LINDA, SYDNEY *and* BROD *enter*.)

LINDA: Do we matter?

SYDNEY: (*With his manuscript*) We certainly do. This isn't just an article, Linda. It's going to be a book. And when it's finished I shall dedicate it to you.

LINDA: Yes? To the wall on which I bounced my ball. To the tree against which I cocked my leg.

SYDNEY: Linda. I shan't be an insurance man any more. I shall be a literary figure. You'll be the wife of a famous man.

HERMANN K: (*Gleefully*) Oh no she won't.

SYDNEY: Well, not famous exactly, but . . .

HERMANN K: Not famous *at all*. Because there isn't going to be an article. There isn't going to be a book.

SYDNEY: But . . . why not?

HERMANN K: Because I've decided to come clean. I'm every bit as bad as the books made me out. Worse.

SYDNEY: I don't understand.

HERMANN K: You're an insurance man. You must be familiar with false claims. This was a false claim. Both parties were lying.

KAFKA: Father.

HERMANN K: Shut your face, you wet dishcloth.

LINDA: I knew you were lying.

SYDNEY: But why deceive me?

HERMANN K: I'm human. Just. I wanted to be liked.

LINDA: (*To* KAFKA) But why did you lie?

HERMANN K: Blackmail.

KAFKA: Dad!

HERMANN K: Don't you Dad me, you dismal Jimmy. Do you want to know how I made him toe the line?

KAFKA: You promised!

HERMANN K: You know me: I'm your terrible father. When did I ever keep a promise? Besides, I owe it to posterity. I don't know how to put this delicately . . .

BROD: It's never been a problem before.

(KAFKA *puts his hands over his ears.*)

HERMANN K: The long and short of it is: my son is ashamed of his old man.

BROD: We know that. That's what all the books say, starting with mine.

HERMANN K: No, not me. He's ashamed of his old man.

KAFKA: Don't listen. Please don't listen.

HERMANN K: Putting it bluntly: his old man doesn't compare with his old man's old man. His. Mine. (*He makes an unequivocal gesture.*)

SYDNEY: But I know that. Everyone knows that.

LINDA: Even I know that.

KAFKA: You? How?

SYDNEY: (*Finding the book*) *Dreams, Life and Literature*. A study of Kafka by Hall and Lind, University Press, North Carolina.

LINDA: So you see, your private parts have long been public property.

KAFKA: He's won again. When will it ever stop?

HERMANN K: Stop? Stop? Mr World Famous Writer with the Small Dick, it won't ever stop. Literature goes on. You are one of its big heroes and I am one its small villains.

LINDA: I'm a little confused.

BROD: That's nothing fresh.

LINDA: You didn't like your son?

HERMANN K: No.

LINDA: But then you said you did.

HERMANN K: Yes.

LINDA: And now you say you didn't.

HERMANN K: Yes.

LINDA: Sydney (*Pause.*) Is that what they mean by Kafka-esque?

HERMANN K: I thought I wanted to be a good father.

LINDA: Yes.

HERMANN K: Now I don't.

LINDA: Why?

HERMANN K: Because, *snowdrop*, a good father is a father you forget.

BROD: You had a good father. You haven't forgotten him.

HERMANN K: I have.

BROD: But he could . . .

LINDA and HERMANN K: (*Together*) . . . lift a sack of potatoes with his teeth.

HERMANN K: Yes. But that's *all* I can remember about him. Whereas bad fathers are never forgotten. They jump out of the wardrobe. They hide under the bed. They come on as policemen. Sons never get rid of them. So long as my son's famous, I'm famous. I figure in all the biographies, I get invited to all the parties. I'm a bad father, so I'm in the text.

BROD: Same old Hermann.

HERMANN K: Anyway I couldn't change things now. My accountant would never forgive me.

61

(HERMANN K *goes.* FATHER *just misses him as he goes.*)

FATHER: Has he gone? Damn. I was wanting to bring him abreast of the latest turnaround in Kafka studies. Whereas we have all been brought up to suppose that Kafka and his father were at daggers drawn, recent research has revealed that they both got on famously.

BROD: Wrong.

FATHER: You can't have me taken away when I'm in touch with the latest developments in Kafka studies. What did you say?

LINDA: You're wrong.

FATHER: No. No. You're trying to confuse me. They were like you and me – friends.

SYDNEY: No, Dad. They couldn't stand one another.

FATHER: I give up. Put me away. My limited studies of Kafka have convinced me that being a vegetable is not without its attractions. (*He retires.*)

KAFKA: Thank God I was never a father. It's the one achievement nobody can take away.

BROD: You don't need to have children in order to be a father. You were so dedicated to writing, so set on expressing yourself even if it killed you, which it eventually did, that, like the best and worst of fathers, you have been an example and a reproach to writers ever since. Take him. (*Meaning* SYDNEY.) He loves you. He hates you. So do I.

LINDA: You're not sorry?

BROD: How should I be sorry? If I hadn't been Kafka's friend I wouldn't have been in the play.

SYDNEY: If you hadn't been Kafka's friend there would have been no play. There would have been no Kafka.

(KAFKA *is about to speak.*)

BROD: Now don't say it.

(KAFKA *puts his hand on* BROD's *shoulder and smiles.*)
Be content. We will meet at that posthumous cocktail party, posterity. (BROD *goes.*)

KAFKA: Shall we see you there?

LINDA: Who says we'll be invited?

SYDNEY: (*Picking up the manuscript*) This is our invitation.

LINDA: Is it? Fifteen thousand books and articles about Kafka.

What's one more? Poor Sydney. Anyway, you hate parties.

SYDNEY: This one might be different.

LINDA: That's what one always thinks, every, every time.

KAFKA: You are so like Dora.

LINDA: Enjoy yourself. Be miserable.

KAFKA: I will. You know me.

(*They touch fingers as they touched before.* KAFKA *vanishes.*)

SYDNEY: You see, try as we will, we can never quite touch Kafka. He always eludes us. We never do know him.

LINDA: I know him better than you.

SYDNEY: Really? So what's this? (*He takes the quiche out of the bookcase.*)

LINDA: (*Hurt*) His lunch. My quiche. Oh, Sydney.

SYDNEY: (*Consoling her*) I'll eat it.

(*They share it.*)

LINDA: Who was Dora?

SYDNEY: His last girlfriend. The only one who made him happy. She got him to eat, wrap up warm. Nursed him, I suppose. She wasn't interested in his work at all. When he told her to burn some of it, she did. (*Pause.*) You'd better burn this, I suppose. (*He gives her his manuscript.*)

LINDA: Are you sure?

SYDNEY: Yes.

(*She gathers it up briskly and is going.*)

Wait. What do you think?

LINDA: Since when does it matter what I think? (*She is going again.*)

SYDNEY: Linda. Do *you* think I should burn it?

LINDA: How do I know?

SYDNEY: Will you read it?

LINDA: That depends. I may not have time. Now Father's off our hands I'm going back to nursing. (*Pause.*) Anyway, I couldn't have burned it.

(SYDNEY *is touched. She hands back the manuscript.*)

We're in a smokeless zone.

SYDNEY: You're not stupid.

LINDA: No. After all, I know that Auden never wore underpants and Mr Right for E. M. Forster was an Egyptian tramdriver.

Only some day I'll learn the bits in between.

SYDNEY: (*A cry of despair*) Oh Linda. There's no need. This is England. In England facts like that pass for culture. Gossip is the acceptable face of intellect.

LINDA: What I don't understand, she said, like the secretary in the detective story when the loose ends are being tied up, what I still don't understand is why people are so interested in a writer's life in the first place.

SYDNEY: You like fairy stories.

LINDA: If they have happy endings.

SYDNEY: This one does, every, every, time. We are reading a book. A novel, say, or a book of short stories. It interests us because it is new, because it is . . . novel, so we read on. And yet in what we call our heart of hearts (which is the part that is heartless) we know that like children we prefer the familiar stories, the tales we have been told before. And there is one story we never fail to like because it is always the same. The myth of the artist's life. How one struggled for years against poverty and indifference only to die and find himself famous. Another is a prodigy finding his way straight to the public's heart to be loved and celebrated while still young, but paying the price by dying and being forgotten. Or just dying.

(*During the following the lights concentrate on* SYDNEY *and music starts in the distance.*)

This one is a hermit, that one a hellraiser, but the myth can accommodate them all, no variation on it, but it is familiar even to someone who has never read a book. He plunges from a bridge and she hits the bottle. Both of them *paid*. That is the myth. Art is not a gift, it is a transaction, and somewhere an account has to be settled. It may be in the gas oven, in front of a train or even at the altar, but on this side of the grave or that settled it must be. We like to be told, you see, that you can't win. We prefer artists to die poor and forgotten, like Rembrandt, Mozart or Beethoven, none of whom did, quite. One reason why Kafka is so celebrated is because his life conforms in every particular to what we have convinced ourselves an artist's life should be. Destined to write, he dispenses with love, with fame and finally with life

64

itself so that it seems at the very last he has utterly failed. But we know that in the fairy story this is what always happens to the hero just before his ultimate triumph. It is not the end. (SYDNEY *and* LINDA *go. As the lights come up we are in heaven, which is a big party going on offstage.* KAFKA *enters through the french windows, which have become the Pearly Gates, and finds the* RECORDING ANGEL, *played by* BROD.)

KAFKA: I don't know what I'm doing here. I shouldn't be in Heaven.

RECORDING ANGEL: Good. That proves you're in the right place.

KAFKA: I don't feel I deserve it.

RECORDING ANGEL: That proves you do. The worse you feel, the better you are, that's the celestial construct.

KAFKA: Will I be allowed to be as despairing here as I was on earth?

RECORDING ANGEL: You can be as gloomy as you like so long as it makes you happy. Look at Ibsen. He can just about manage a smile for Strindberg but nobody else. Now who don't you know? The gentleman over there with the shocking beard, that's Dostoevsky. Who's he talking to? Oh. Noël Coward! They've got a lot of ground to cover. There's Wittgenstein and Betty Hutton. Got it together at last! There's Proust (Hi, Marcel!) trying to con one of the waiters into making him a cup of tea so that he can do his act. (Kissy kissy!) Oh, and there's the Virgin Mary.

KAFKA: She looks sad.

RECORDING ANGEL: She's never got over not having grandchildren. I say to her, well, look on the bright side. What about Gothic architecture? With two thousand years of Christianity to your credit what are grandchildren? But, as she said to me in a moment of confidence, 'You can't knit bootees for the Nicene Creed.'

KAFKA: Are there Jews here?

RECORDING ANGEL: *Mais oui!* In droves.

KAFKA: And there's no quota?

RECORDING ANGEL: Not officially. Though God is quite keen on them, naturally.

KAFKA: I was fond of animals. Are they here?

65

RECORDING ANGEL: Sorry, love. No animals. Well, they don't have a moral life.

KAFKA: No mice, beetles or birds?

RECORDING ANGEL: No. But if St Francis of Assisi can get used to it, I'm sure you can. You didn't really like them anyway. They were only metaphors. No metaphors here. No allegory. And nobody says 'hopefully' or 'at the end of the day' or 'at this moment in time'. We're in a presence-of-God situation here, you see. Talk of the devil, here comes God.

(GOD, *who is, of course,* HERMANN K, *enters.*)

GOD: My son!

KAFKA: Who are you?

GOD: Well, I'm all sorts of things. The BBC. The *Oxford English Dictionary*. The Queen. The Ordnance Survey Map. Anything with a bit of authority really.

KAFKA: You're my father.

GOD: Of course. What did you expect? Enjoying yourself?

KAFKA: No. It's like a terrible party.

GOD: It is a party. And I'm the Host. (*He should plainly be itching to dance, looking over his son's shoulder and waving at other – invisible – guests, all the time he's talking.*) There's Gandhi. Go easy on the cheese straws, Mahatma! You're going to have to watch that waistline! Can you dance?

KAFKA: No.

GOD: I can. Mind you, I can do everything. Nuclear physics, the samba . . . it's all one to me.

KAFKA: Oh, God.

GOD: Yes? Come on. Just be happy you're invited. I bet you never thought you'd see Leonard Woolf doing the cha-cha.

(SYDNEY *crosses, dancing.*)

SYDNEY: I'm not doing the cha-cha. It's Virginia. She's just put a hot cocktail sausage down my neck.

GOD: (*Calling after him*) You could have fooled me, Len. He couldn't, of course. I know it all.

KAFKA: Father. Did you ever get round to reading my books?

GOD: Are you still on about that? No, of course not. No fiction here anyway. No writing. No literature. No art. No need. After all what were they? Echoes, imitations. This is the real

thing. Son. Try not to disappoint me this time. And there's
no shortage of time. We're here for ever, you and me.

KAFKA: Yes, Father.

GOD: Listen, unless I'm very much mistaken (and that's a
theological nonsense) that sounds to me like the rumba and
I've promised it to Nurse Cavell.

(LINDA *comes on in a nurse's costume but with Carmen Miranda
headgear.*)

KAFKA: Nurse Cavell didn't look like Carmen Miranda.

GOD: I know. Why do you think they shot her?

(FATHER *has come on, playing the maracas.*)

And now, as the magic fingers of Bertrand Russell beat out a
mad mazurka on the maracas, I must go and move in my
well-known mysterious way. *Ciao,* son.

KAFKA: *Ciao,* Father.

(*The music swells as* GOD *and* LINDA *dance. The stage is
suddenly dark and* KAFKA *comes forward.*)

I'll tell you something. Heaven is going to be hell.

THE INSURANCE MAN
A play for television

Diary
July–August 1985

The Insurance Man is set in Prague. It begins in 1945 with the city on the eve of liberation by the Russians, though the main events of the story, told in flashback, take place before the First World War. The film was shot in Bradford, where every other script I've written seems to have been shot, and also in Liverpool, a city I didn't know and had never worked in. Bradford was chosen because among the few buildings the city has elected to preserve are some nineteenth-century warehouses behind the cathedral. From the nationality of the merchants orginally trading there this neighbourhood is known locally as Little Germany. The trade has gone but the buildings remain, the exteriors now washed and sandblasted but the interiors much as they were when the last bolt of cloth was despatched in the 1960s. Liverpool likewise has many empty buildings and for the same reason, and there we had an even wider choice. I found both places depressing, Liverpool in particular. Work though it is, a play, however serious, is play, and play seems tactless where there is no work.

Tuesday, 9 July, Connaught Rooms, Bradford
These masonic chambers on what's left of Manningham Lane serve as part of the Workers Accident Insurance Institute, the office in Prague where Kafka was a conscientious and well-thought-of executive. It is only the first day of shooting and already I feel somewhat spare. We are filming scenes in the lift, which is just large enough to contain the actors and the camera crew. There's no hope of hearing the dialogue so I sit on a window sill and read, wishing, after writing nearly a score of films, that I didn't still feel it necessary to be in attendance at the birth. Just below where we are filming is Valley Parade, Bradford City's football ground where two months ago dozens of fans perished in a fire. Glance down a back street and there is the blackened gateway.

Wednesday, 10 July, Holcraft Castings and Forgings, Thornbury
Periodically between 1911 and 1917 Kafka helped to manage an

asbestos factory set up by his brother-in-law. The hero of *The Insurance Man* is Franz, a young man who contracts a mysterious skin disease, seemingly from his job in a dyeworks. As a result he is sacked and comes to the Workers Accident Insurance Institute to claim compensation. He fails, but Kafka, anxious to do him a good turn, offers him a job in his brother-in-law's asbestos factory. The story is told in flashback thirty years later when Franz, now an old man, comes to his doctor to be told that Kafka's good turn has sealed his death warrant. Kafka describes in his diary the dust in the original asbestos factory and how, when they came off shift, the girls would dash it from their overalls in clouds. Even so I feel the design department has overdone it: dust coats every surface and lies in drifts against the machinery. I mention this to Richard Eyre, wondering if it's a little too much. It turns out we have had nothing to do with it: the forge, shut down six months ago, is just as it was.

The offices too have not been touched, a ledger open on a desk, records and files still on the shelves. In a locker is a cardigan and three polystyrene plates, remnants of a last takeaway and taped to the door a yellowing cyclostyled letter dated 12 June 1977. It is from a Mr Goff, evidently an executive of the firm, living at The Langdales, Kings Grove, Bingley. Mr Goff has been awarded the OBE in the Jubilee Honours and in the letter he expresses the hope 'that the People, who are the Main Prop in any endeavour, many with great skill and ability, will take Justification and Pride in it and will', he earnestly hopes, 'feel that they will be sharing in the Honour conferred on me'.

Thursday, 11 July, Downs, Coulter and Co., Vicar Lane, Bradford
Another empty factory, this time an ex-textile manufacturers, which we fit out as the office and medical room of a dyeworks. On the wall is a list of internal telephone numbers: Mr Jack, Mr Ben, Mr Jim, Mr Luke. It has evidently been a family firm and sounds straight out of The Crowthers of Bankdam. No wonder it did not survive long into Mrs Thatcher's England. Also on the wall is an advertising calendar sent out by Chas Walker and Sons, Beta Works, Leeds, and headed *Textile Town Holidays 1974*. From big cities like Leeds and Manchester down to the smallest woollen

and cotton towns like Tottington and Clayton le Moors, the calendar lists the different fortnights in the summer the mills would close down. If they hadn't closed down for good already, that is. The artwork is a fanciful drawing of a toreador watched by elegant couples under Martini umbrellas but the obstinate echoes are of men in braces sat in deck chairs, fat ladies paddling at Bridlington and Flamborough and Whitley Bay. For most of them now one long holiday.

Tuesday, 16 July, Bradford

A boy of sixteen, hair streaked and dressed in the fashion, leads an old lady down Bridge Street. In this town of the unemployed he is probably her home help or on some community care scheme so it's not just the spectacle of youthful goodness that makes it touching. But not yet of an age to go arm in arm he is leading her by the hand. He little more than a child, she a little less, they go hand in hand along Hall Ings in the morning sunshine.

Night Shoot, Little Germany

In the original script the first scene was set in the doctor's surgery in Prague at the end of the war. Old Franz is let in and mentions there is a body hanging from the lamp-post outside. Richard Eyre thought that a more arresting opening would be of Franz picking his way down the bombed street and hanging in the foreground the man's body.

The corpse is played by an extra, who is perhaps sixty. It is a complicated shot, done at night and involves water flooding down the street, the camera on a crane and high above it another much taller crane, a 'cherry-picker', from which (since the lamp-post is false) the 'corpse' has to be suspended. There is no dialogue and nothing for me to do. It's too dark to read and too cold to be standing about. We have done the first shot when I notice that a placard has been hung round the corpse's neck saying TRAITOR. I think this is too specific and ask Richard if we can do a shot without it. There are other technical problems to be sorted out before we do a second take and those not involved hang around chatting and drinking coffee. As so often on a film the atmosphere is one of boredom and resignation, troops waiting for the action. Or the 'Action'.

Suddenly there is a commotion at the lamp-post. The hanging man has been sick, is unconscious. There is a rush to get him down, many hands reaching up, the scene, in our carefully contrived light and shade like a Descent from the Cross. Thankful at last to have something to do the duty policeman briskly calls up an ambulance while the make-up girls (odd that this is part of their function) chafe the man's feet. At first it is feared that he has had a heart attack but soon he is sitting up. We abandon the shot and Mervyn, the production manager, calls a wrap. The water is turned off, props begin to clear the rubble from the street as an ambulance arrives and the patient gets in under his own steam. There is some discussion whether anyone from the unit should go with him, as someone undoubtedly should. But it is 3.30 a.m. and he goes off in the ambulance alone. I note my own reluctance to assume this responsibility. I could have gone, though there is no reason why I should. Except that it's my play. I'm to blame for him hanging there in the first place. (Though it seems fairly obvious to me, in the finished film the meaning of this hanged man puzzles some people. The doctor has heard the man running down the street the previous night, trying to find a refuge from his pursuers. He bangs on a door and it is opened – by his pursuers. His refuge turns out to be his doom. This kind of paradox is one associated with Kafka and it's also the paradox at the heart of the play. Kafka does Franz a favour by giving him a job in his factory, but since the factory turns out to make asbestos this good turn leads in the end to Franz's death.)

Wednesday, 17 July, Peckover Street, Little Germany
Dan Day-Lewis, who plays Kafka, has a stooping, stiff-necked walk which I take to be part of his characterization. It's certainly suited to the role and may be derived from the exact physical description of Kafka given by Gustav Janouch. Even so I'm not sure if the walk is Kafka or Dan since he's so conscientious he seldom comes out of character between takes and I never see him walking otherwise.

We film the scenes between Kafka and his father (Dave King), the Kafka family home set up on another floor of the same empty warehouse. When I first worked on the script with Richard Eyre

74

he wondered whether these scenes of the Kafka household were necessary, feeling that the film is really the story of Franz to which Kafka is only incidental. I pressed for them then, the producer Innes Lloyd agreed, so here we are in the Kafka apartment. Any doubts are resolved by a scene in which Hermann Kafka gets into his son's bed, then stands on it (an image taken from one of Kafka's stories) and begins to bounce up and down, the sound that of the sexual intercourse Kafka could often hear from his parents' bedroom when he was struggling to write.

(Richard's instinct proves right, nevertheless: in the editing the scene is cut as it seems to hold up the story.)

The Bradford sequences over we now have three days off before moving to Liverpool.

Tuesday, 23 July, Fruit Exchange, Victoria Street, Liverpool
This is a great rarity, a location that exactly matches the scene as I imagined it. A small steeply raked auditorium with a gallery done in light oak and lit by five leaded windows. It was built in 1900 and is as pleasing and nicely proportioned as a Renaissance theatre. Each seat is numbered, the numbers carved in a wood that matches the pews and facing them a podium on which is the hydraulic lift that brought up the produce to be auctioned. Ben Whitrow stands on the podium now as we wait to rehearse a scene in which, as a professor of medicine, he uses Franz in a clinical demonstration for his students. The students are played by fifty Liverpool boys, some of whom are given lines to speak. ('What is this word?' asks one. 'Origin.' 'What does that mean?') One is tempted to think that this auditorium and another that adjoins it should be rehabilitated and used as theatres. For revues possibly. Seeing it for the first time Vivian Pickles remarks, 'Look out! I feel a song coming on.' Yet if it was a theatre it would straightaway lose its charm, part of which lies in its being unwanted, a find. We do our little bit to hasten its decline by cutting out one section of the pews to accommodate a gallery. Pledged to restore it to its original state, our carpenters will patch it up but it will never be quite the same.

In the scene Robert Hines, who plays Franz, has to stand naked on the podium under the bored eyes of fifty medical students. As the day wears on the extras have no problem simulating boredom, often having to be woken for the take. I never fail to be impressed by the bravery of actors. Robert is a striking and elegant figure, seemingly unselfconscious about his nakedness. Did I have to display myself in front of a total stranger, let alone fifty of them, my part would shrink to the size of an acorn. Robert's remains unaffected. I mention this to John Pritchard, the sound supervisor. 'I see,' he says drily. 'You subscribe to the theory of the penis as seaweed.' It later transpires that Robert's seeming equanimity has been achieved only after drinking a whole bottle of wine.

Wednesday, 24 July, St George's Hall, Liverpool
We film a long and complicated shot that introduces the Workers Accident Insurance Institute, the office where Kafka worked for most of his life. I had written this shot in several scenes but Richard Eyre combines them into one five-minute tracking shot. An office girl is making her rounds, collecting on behalf of the retiring Head of Department. The camera goes with her as she moves from office to office, calling in turn on the three clerks who figure in the story, finally ending up in Kafka's office, where he is dictating to his secretary.

The WAI office has been built in the St George's Hall, the massive municipal temple on the Plateau at the heart of Liverpool. Ranged round the vast hall are statues of worthies from the great days of the city and on the floor a rich and elaborate mosaic, set with biblical homilies. 'By thee kings reign and princes decree justice,' say the roundels on the floor. 'Save the NHS. Keep Contractors Out,' say other roundels, badges stuck there at a recent People's Festival. 'He hath given me skill that He might be honoured,' says the floor. 'Save the pits,' say the stickers. It is a palimpsest of our industrial history. Peel and George Stephenson look down.

Most of the unit are staying in the Adelphi, a once grand hotel and the setting of the thirties' comedy, *Grand National Night*. More recently the vast lounge figured in the television version of *Brideshead Revisited* as the interior of a transatlantic liner. One gets a hint of its former grandeur in the size of the towels but the service is not what it was. At breakfast I ask for some brown toast. The waiter, a boy of about sixteen and as thin as a Cruikshank cartoon, hesitates for a moment then slopes over the breakfast bar and riffles through a basket of toast. Eventually he returns with two darkish pieces of white toast. 'Are these brown enough?' It is not a joke.

Friday, 26 July, St George's Hall
At the centre of the gilded grilles on the huge doors of the St George's Hall is the motto SPQL – the senate and people of Liverpool. There isn't a senate now and the building serves no civic function, the courts, which once it housed, transferred to less noble concrete premises down the hill. As for the people, they occasionally figure at rallies and suchlike and marches seem to begin here, but the portico stinks of urine and grass grows on the steps.

In front of the St George's Hall is a war memorial, a stone of remembrance inlaid with bronze reliefs. The inscription reads: OUT THE NORTH PARTS A GREAT COMPANY AND A MIGHTY ARMY. The panels, soldiers on one side, civilians on the other, are vaguely Vorticist in inspiration, the figures formal and angular and all inclined at the same slant. It was designed by Professor Lionel Budden of Liverpool University and the bronze reliefs done by H. Tyson Smith. These aren't notable names but it is a noble thing, far more so than Lutyens's Whitehall Cenotaph.

Behind the war memorial one looks across the Plateau to the Waterloo Monument and a perfect group of nineteenth-century buildings; the library, the Walker Art Gallery and the Court of Sessions. Turn a little further and the vista is ruined by the new TGWU building, which looks like a G-Plan chest of drawers. A blow from the Left. Look the other way and there's a slap from the Right – the even more awful St John's Centre. Capitalism and ideology combine to ruin a majestic city.

Tony Haygarth plays Pohlmann, the kindly clerk in Kafka's office. In his period suit he is hanging about the steps at lunchtime wanting company. 'I'd like to go over to the pub, you see, but in this outfit I'd feel a bit *left-handed*.'

Sunday, 28 July, Cunard Building
Kafka was once standing outside the Workers Accident Insurance

Institute watching the claimants going in. 'How modest these people are,' he remarked to Max Brod. 'Instead of storming the building and smashing everything to bits they come to us and plead.' We film that scene today with the injured workers thronging up the steps. Most of them are made up to look disabled but a couple of them genuinely are – a fair young man with one arm who plays one of the commissionaires and a boy with one leg and a squashed ear, who like the lame boy in the Pied Piper comes limping along at the tail of the crowd. Without regarding the disabled as a joke I have put jokes on the subject into the script. 'Just because you've got one leg,' shouts an official, 'doesn't mean you can behave like a wild beast.' Though the intention is to emphasize the heartlessness of the officials and the desperation of the injured workpeople the presence of these genuine cripples shows one up as equally heartless. I can't imagine, have not tried to imagine, what it is like to have a limb torn off or have half an ear. 'You say you understand,' says Franz in the film, 'but if you do and you do nothing about it then you're worse than the others. You're evil.' This is an echo of Kafka's own remark that to write is to do the devil's work. And to say that it is the devil's work does not excuse it. One glibly despises the photographer who zooms in on the starving child or the dying soldier without offering help. Writing is not different.

Monday, 28 July
It is nine o'clock and still light and I go looking for a restaurant to have my supper. I walk through the terrible St John's Centre. It has a restaurant, set on a concrete pole (may the architect rot); now empty, it boasts a tattered notice three hundred feet up advertising to passing seagulls that it is TO LET. I pass three children, the eldest about twelve. They are working on a shop window which has CLOSING DOWN painted on it. Spelling obviously not their strong point, they are standing back from it puzzling how they can turn it into an obscenity when I pass with my book. The book takes their eye and there's bit of 'Look at him. He's got a book.' 'What's your book?' I walk on and find myself in an empty precinct. The children have stopped taunting and seem to have disappeared. I look round and find that the trio are silently

78

keeping pace with me. In an utterly empty square they are no more than three feet away. I am suddenly alarmed, stop and turn back to where there are more people. I have never done that in England and not even in New York.

Tuesday, 30 July, St George's Hall
Bob the gaffer is giving one of the sparks directions over a faulty lamp. 'Kill it before you strike it,' he says. It is a remark that could be called Kafkaesque did not the briefest acquaintance with the character of Kafka discourage one from using the word. But he lives and goes by public transport: at a bus-stop today the graffiti: HOPE IS FUCKING HOPELESS.

Wednesday, 31 July, St George's Hall
Happy to be drawing towards the end of the shoot, I have come to dislike Liverpool. Robert Ross said that Dorsetshire rustics, after Hardy, had the insolence of the artist's model and so it is with Liverpudlians. They have figured in too many plays and have a cockiness that comes from being told too often that they and their city are special. The accent doesn't help. There is a rising inflexion in it, particularly at the end of a sentence, that gives even the most formal exchange a built-in air of grievance. They all have the chat and it laces every casual encounter, everybody wanting to do you their little verbal dance. One such is going on at hotel reception tonight as I wait for my key. 'You don't know me,' says a drunken young man to the receptionist, 'but I'm a penniless millionaire.' You don't know me, but I'm a fifty-one-year-old playwright anxious to get to my bed.

Thursday, 1 August, Examination Schools, University of Liverpool
In St George's Hall we have been insulated against noise. The vastness of the building meant that even a violent thunderstorm did not interrupt filming, the only problem the muffling of its huge echo. This final location is different. Outside three roads meet and the bus station is nearby so that traffic makes filming almost impossible. As chairman of the tribunal Geoffrey Palmer has a long, passionate speech, his only scene in the film. Traffic noise means that we go for take after take before we get one that

the sound department thinks is even passable. Then, between buses, we re-record the scene sentence by sentence, sometimes even phrase by phrase. It is an actor's nightmare as all feeling has to be sacrificed to achieve consistency of tone. Entitled to get cross, Geoffrey Palmer remains good-humoured and in complete control and when the speech is edited there is no hint of the conditions under which it was recorded. A splendid actor with an absolutely deadpan face, he is an English Walter Matthau.

Monday, 5 August
The guard, an elderly and distinguished-looking West Indian, announces over the Tannoy that this is the 16.45 from Leeds to Kings Cross, the estimated time of arrival 19.15. He adds 'May the presence of the Lord Jesus Christ be with you and keep you always if you will let him. Thank you.' Nobody smiles.

Friday, 9 August, London
Dr McGregor sends me for an X-ray to UCH and I go down to Gower Street to make the appointment. I stand at the Enquiry Desk while the plump, unsmiling receptionist elaborately finishes what she is doing before turning her attention to me.

'Yes?' She glances at my form. 'Second floor.'

I long to drag her across the counter and shake her till her dentures drop out. 'Listen,' I want to say, 'you are as essential to the well-being of this hospital as its most exalted consultant. You can do more for the spirits of patients coming to this institution than the most skilful surgeon. Just by being nice. Be *nice*, you cow.'

I sit upstairs waiting for the next receptionist and realize that this is what we have been acting out, playing at these last two weeks in Liverpool. Here I am with my form, queuing with my docket as we have filmed the claimants queuing with theirs in Prague in 1910. I note that even when we were filming and playing at bureaucracy we fell into its traps. I never had much to do with the extras. I mixed with the actors, who were known to me and who played the officials, the named parts. I kept my distance from the throng of claimants, none of whose names or faces I knew. Indeed I resented them just as the real-life officials must have done and for the same reasons: they crowded the place out, mobbed the coffee urn and generally made life difficult. Well, I reflect, now I am punished.

It is a feature of institutions that the permanent staff resent those for whose benefit the institution exists. And so it will go on, even beyond the grave. I have no doubt that in heaven the angels will regard the blessed as a necessary evil.

The Insurance Man was first broadcast on BBC2 on 23 February 1986. The cast was as follows:

FRANZ (OLD)	Trevor Peacock
DOCTOR	Alan MacNaughtan
FRANZ (YOUNG)	Robert Hines
LANDLADY	Diana Rayworth
OLD MAN IN DYEWORKS	Teddy Turner
WORKMEN	Phil Hearne
	Bernard Wrigley
FACTORY DOCTOR	Ronan Wilmot
NURSE	Jill Frudd
BEATRICE	Katy Behean
UNDERMANAGER	C. J. Allen
FOREMAN	Fred Gaunt
CHRISTINA	Tessa Wojtczak
CHRISTINA'S FATHER	Johnny Allen
CHRISTINA'S MOTHER	Margo Stanley
CHRISTINA'S GRANDMOTHER	Judith Nelmes
CHRISTINA'S SISTER	Fran O'Shea
DOORMAN	Bill Moody
LILY	Vivian Pickles
INQUIRIES CLERK	Guy Nicholls
INQUIRIES OFFICIAL	Alan Starkey
SEAMSTRESS	Charlotte Coleman
COLLECTING GIRL	Oona Kirsch
POHLMANN	Tony Haygarth
GUTLING	Jim Broadbent
JAM WORKER	David Miller
CULICK	Hugh Fraser
HEAD-BANDAGED WORKMAN	Ted Carroll
HEAD OF DEPARTMENT	Nicholas Selby
HEAD CLERK	Richard Kane
KAFKA	Daniel Day Lewis
MISS WEBER	Rosemary Martin
BUTCHER BOY	Lee Daley

LIMPING CLIENT	John de Frates
TALL WOMAN	Richenda Carey
ONE-LEGGED MAN	Sam Kelly
MAN WITHOUT EAR	Kenny Ireland
ATTENDANT IN WAITING ROOM	Ted Beyer
BALD MAN	Iggy Navarro
WOMAN IN WAITING ROOM	Rosemary Chamney
MAN IN WAITING ROOM	Peter Christian
THE ANGRY DOCTOR	Geoffrey Palmer
THE THIN DOCTOR	Ralph Nossek
THE FAT DOCTOR	Roger Hammond
WOMAN AT TRIBUNAL	Joanne Ellis
FRANZ'S FATHER	Derry Power
LECTURER IN MEDICAL SCHOOL	Benjamin Whitrow
MAN WITH STOMACH HOLE	Billy Moores
YOUNG WOMAN IN MEDICAL SCHOOL	Deborah Langley
KAFKA'S BROTHER-IN-LAW	Toby Salaman
Designer	Geoff Powell
Photography	Nat Crosby
Music	Ilona Sekacz
Producer	Innes Lloyd
Director	Richard Eyre

EXT. STREET. NIGHT
*A foreign city. A body hangs from a lamp-post. In the distance the
sound of gunfire and bombs falling.* FRANZ (OLD) *walks down the
street past the hanging body to ring the bell at a block of apartments.*

INT. DOCTOR'S CONSULTING ROOM, PRAGUE. NIGHT. 1945
*An X-ray plate of a pair of damaged lungs. The X-ray fills the screen.
Over it we hear the distant sound of bombs falling. Superimposed on
the screen over the X-ray plate:* Prague, 1945. *We see as we pull out
that the X-ray plate is being examined by an oldish* DOCTOR *in a
once well-to-do consulting room. The* DOCTOR *is in an overcoat, and
it is night. The state of the lungs on the plate obviously depresses him.
He shakes his head. A doorbell rings.*

DOCTOR: (*Calling*) Lotte! Lotte! (*Listens, calls again:*) Lotte!
(*When there is no response he gets up to answer the door himself.
He goes out and we hear him open the outside door to admit a
patient. The outside door closes again.* DOCTOR *and* PATIENT
ascend the stairs.)
(*Out of vision*) My housekeeper must be in the cellar. (*Into
vision*) What is it like breathing?

FRANZ: Well . . . we've been having some cold weather.

DOCTOR: No pain?

FRANZ: Not pain as you'd call pain. In peacetime you might call
it pain. These days illness is a luxury. They've hung
somebody from your lamp-post.

DOCTOR: Last night. Still. We don't want to lose *you*, do we?
(*The remark sounds absurd in the light of someone hanged from
the lamp-post outside and there is a pause. The* DOCTOR *and*
FRANZ *come into the consulting room. Both are in their sixties.*)
Sit down. Get your breath back.
(*He gets him a drink out of a cabinet. From the way he pours it,
it is obviously precious.*)

FRANZ: (*Indicating the drink*) Does this mean bad news?
(*The* DOCTOR *smiles.*)

DOCTOR: We might as well drink it. Before the Russians do.
(*The patient,* FRANZ, *is a plain-spoken man but he has done
quite well in life. The* DOCTOR *pauses.*)

FRANZ: Was it what you suspected?

DOCTOR: (*Lying*) Don't know. Never had the X-ray. Infirmary got cut off. (*Shrugs.*) Still . . . I'm pretty sure it's what I said it was, just a fibrous condition of the lungs. Nothing malignant.

FRANZ: So I'm not going to die.

(*There is a loud crump in the distance as a bomb explodes.*)

DOCTOR: You have to live long enough to be able to die. No. You could go on for years. You could be lucky and live to be hung from a lamp-post.

FRANZ: Funny, you come along thinking this is the Day of Judgement and it never is.

DOCTOR: Or it always is. Tell me, out of sheer curiosity, what other jobs have you done, apart from the railway?

FRANZ: Apart from the railway? Nothing. I started as a porter, I ended up stationmaster of the Central Station.

DOCTOR: Nothing else?

FRANZ: I was in a dyeworks once. For about five minutes.

DOCTOR: A dyeworks?

FRANZ: When I was young. We're talking about before the First War now. Terrible place. It's funny. I thought I was a goner then.

INT. A ROOM IN A CHEAP LODGING HOUSE. EARLY MORNING. 1910.

FRANZ *as a young man lying in bed awake.*

FRANZ (OLD): (*Voice over*) I'd just got engaged and I woke up one fine morning and found there was a strange patch on my skin.

(*He gets up and stands naked in front of the mirror, looking at something on his chest that we do not see. He frowns. There is a picture of a young woman on the dressing-table. There is a very quiet knock on the door. FRANZ clutches his clothes to him.*)

FRANZ (YOUNG): Don't come in.

LANDLADY: (*Out of vision*) Why?

(*We see the door open and a cup and saucer appear round the edge of the door, followed by the LANDLADY, carrying a coffee pot in the other hand.*)

You can't show me anything new. My husband was in the
armed forces. (*Pours the coffee.*) I'm not sure I like all this
coming and going last thing at night. You'll need all your
energy to get on in life.
(*She puts the cup down on the dressing-table.*)
FRANZ: We're going to be married.
LANDLADY: (*Going*) This room used to be let to a fully fledged
optician. He was quite alone. He had diplomas.
(*Back in the room* FRANZ *looks glumly in the glass. He moves
the girl's photograph back a little, looks at it, then at his chest.*)

INT. A DYEWORKS. DAY.
FRANZ (OLD) (*Voice over, across change of scene*) I didn't dare tell
my fiancée and to begin with I didn't let on to anybody. I was
just hoping it would go away. Only it didn't; it got worse.
(*Close-up of cloth being dipped in dye bath. Then reveal
dyeworks. A* WORKMAN *comes up to say something to an*
OLD MAN *who is working at the dye bath. We track the*
WORKMAN *walking along the floor of the dyeworks, followed
by an* OLD MAN. *They come through the works, and the*
OLD MAN *goes into a lavatory while the* WORKMAN *keeps*
cave *outside.*)
OLD MAN: (*Out of vision*) Does it itch?
FRANZ (YOUNG): (*Out of vision*) No.
(*We stay outside until another* WORKMAN *goes in for a piss. We
follow him and see* FRANZ *with the top of his overalls rolled
down, his shirt off and the* OLD MAN *peering at his skin and
belly. All this is watched by the* SECOND WORKMAN, *who is
pissing.*)
OLD MAN: Funny process, dyeing. Saw a lad once, scales from
there down. Ended up spending the whole day in the bath.
Slept in it. That were t'dye. Went to the board with it. They
just pretended it was something in the family.
(*The* OLD MAN *touches the patch of skin with his
dye-discoloured hand. The* OLD MAN *spits.*)
Have you reported it?
(FRANZ *shakes his head.*)
FACTORY DOCTOR: (*Voice over*) Dyeing won't do you any harm . . .

(Cut from the noise of the dyeworks to the relative silence of:)

INT. A CHEAP SURGERY OR MEDICAL ROOM, DYEWORKS.
DAY.
Four or five FACTORY WORKERS *are waiting outside. One has his boot off, which he holds in his hand. Another holds a pad, made of his handkerchief, against some small wound. Others just sit. We follow a* FOREMAN *past them and into the surgery.*
FACTORY DOCTOR: *(Voice over)* . . . Does it itch?
FRANZ: No, sir.
FACTORY DOCTOR: *(In vision, looking as ill as any of the patients)*
    Sore?
FRANZ: No, sir.
FACTORY DOCTOR: Have you been doing something that you
    shouldn't be doing?
FRANZ: No, sir.
FACTORY DOCTOR: *(Mimicking him)* 'No, sir. No, sir.'
    (The FOREMAN *is watching the examination.)*
    Bit on your back. Take off your trousers. Come on.
    (The NURSE *has been taking an interest, while bandaging
    another* PATIENT.)
NURSE: *(Pointing to* FRANZ'*s legs.)* There's some.
FACTORY DOCTOR: Oh, by God. We're all doctors now.
NURSE: His proper skin's lovely.
FRANZ: And it isn't to do with the dye?
FACTORY DOCTOR: Well. Nobody else has it. Don't blame the
    dye. Blame yourself.
    (The DOCTOR *exits.)*
NURSE: He's only young.
    *(*FRANZ *pulls up his trousers and turns to face the* FOREMAN.)

INT. UNDERMANAGER'S OFFICE, DYEWORKS. DAY
An office adjoining the factory floor. We are in the outer office and can see through a dusty window the inner office where the UNDERMANAGER *is talking to the* FOREMAN. *The* UNDERMANAGER *is holding some papers.* FRANZ *sits in the outer office. A pretty secretary,* BEATRICE, *enters with a bunch of cornflowers. She is conscious of* FRANZ *but wary of her boss next door.*

88

BEATRICE: You're insured.
  (FRANZ *looks up, not sure what she's said. She doesn't look at him.*)
  (*Putting flowers in vase*) These are cornflowers. I love blue. You're insured. Ask.
  (*At which point the* UNDERMANAGER *and the* FOREMAN *come into the room, and she goes over to sit at her desk and starts writing in a ledger.*)
UNDERMANAGER: (*Holding a docket*) Take this along to the cashier.
FRANZ: I haven't done anything, sir. What have I done?
UNDERMANAGER: We're not ungenerous. You've got your full bonus.
  (FRANZ *is reluctant to take the docket.*)
FOREMAN: There's generally a whip round.
UNDERMANAGER: Something like that. I've got my other workpeople to consider.
FOREMAN: (*Easing him out*) Come on, lad. Have you got aught in your locker?
  (*They go. The* GIRL's *face is expressionless as she goes on working.*)
UNDERMANAGER: I don't know what he's been doing. I'd've thought it was simple cleanliness.
  (*Suddenly* FRANZ *comes back into the room with the* FOREMAN *trying to stop him.*)
FRANZ: I want to ask about insurance.
  (BEATRICE *rises.*)
FOREMAN: I never said anything.
  (*The* GIRL *has instinctively walked across to open a cupboard door to get a form and the* UNDERMANAGER *catches her movement.*)
UNDERMANAGER: It doesn't apply. Beatrice. It doesn't apply.
  (*She has her hand on the cupboard door.* FRANZ *and* BEATRICE *look at each other.*)

INT. GYMNASIUM. DAY
FRANZ (YOUNG) *is in long trousers, and a singlet. He is exercising on some hanging rings. He checks his chest to see how much of the rash*

shows, then continues to exercise on the hanging rings. He does
beautiful handstands and somersaults on the rings in the gym.
FRANZ (OLD): (*Voice over*) When you're young, you don't give
your body a thought. Now I was thinking about nothing else,
but yet it was as if it didn't belong to me. I wasn't myself any
more.

INT. CHRISTINA'S PARENTS' APARTMENT. NIGHT
A formal supper. FRANZ (YOUNG) *and his fiancée* CHRISTINA
with her PARENTS. *The atmosphere is strained. Nobody is talking.
The family is obviously socially one jump above* FRANZ. *Any
conversation is in undertones. An incongruous note at the dinner table
is an* OLD LADY *who has to be fed. Another* DAUGHTER *puts food
into the* OLD LADY's *mouth.* FRANZ *is trying to hide his diseased
hand and so is trying to eat with just his fork.* CHRISTINA *notices this
just as he crams an overlarge piece of meat into his mouth because he
cannot cut it.*
FATHER: I'm enjoying this, Mother.
MOTHER: Does Franz want some more, Christina?
FATHER: I think he's old enough to speak for himself, Mother,
don't you? One of the family now.
FRANZ (OLD): (*Voice over, above the following dialogue*) I had to
keep my skin to myself – I felt like an animal and I hadn't
told my fiancée I'd lost my job; I daren't.
MOTHER: (*To the other* DAUGHTER *who is feeding the* OLD
LADY) Don't rush her, Rosa. One mouthful at a time.
FATHER: That's right. Just take your time. Take your time. It's
like everything else. Just take your time.
(CHRISTINA *discreetly tries to get* FRANZ *to use his knife but he
ignores her.*)

INT. FRANZ'S LODGING/TUNNEL. NIGHT
Franz's suit hung over the wardrobe mirror. FRANZ (YOUNG) *in
bed, not asleep. We see him reflected in the mirror. Zoom into mirror
and mix to:* FRANZ (YOUNG) *in silhouette walking down a tunnel.*
FRANZ (OLD): (*Voice over*) The girl in the office had given me a

form. She said I had a claim. I had to take the form to the Workers Accident Insurance Institute on Poric Street. Gone now. Though the building's still there. That building!

EXT. OFFICE BLOCK, PORIC STREET, PRAGUE. DAY
A large nineteenth-century office block. The Town Hall clock is striking. The office has steps leading up to the doors. FRANZ (YOUNG) *comes out of the tunnel opposite and joins the throng walking up the stairs on their way into the building. There is one main door and smaller ones on either side. Before the main door is an imposing* DOORMAN.

DOORMAN: (*Shouting to a man on crutches*) Just because you've got one leg doesn't mean you can behave like a wild beast . . . (*To other* CLAIMANTS *who approach him with forms and chits*) Look. I'm not interested in bits of paper. Wipe your feet, wipe your feet. You're not coming into the factory now.
(FRANZ *tries to go in the central door.*)
Oi, this isn't your door. That's your door.
(THE DOORMAN *shoves* FRANZ *in the direction of the other door, while letting the* HEAD OF DEPARTMENT *and* HEAD CLERK *pass through unhindered. He also lets through another official, whom we will later discover to be* KAFKA. *He is treated very deferentially by the* DOORMAN.)
Morning, Herr Doktor.

INT. ENTRANCE HALL/CORRIDOR AND MAIN HALL, OFFICE BLOCK. DAY
We follow FRANZ *into the building, where there is a good deal of bustle.*

DOORMAN: (*Out of vision*) Out of the way. Out of the way.
(*We see* CLERKS *arriving for work,* WORKMEN, *some of them maimed, and* KAFKA *threading his way through and going up some stairs in the background. Among those entering we should see a* BUTCHER'S BOY *with a bandaged hand and other injured parties who will figure later in offices and corridors upstairs, including a man who is utterly bald, a man with one leg, and a woman with a scarred face. They all teem along a*

corridor and enter a huge hall. We follow FRANZ *as a uniformed official points him to a bench just outside an inquiries window. The door of this should go up and down like a rat-trap. Any odd* Alice in Wonderland *features like this should be emphasized. One or two people are sitting waiting outside the inquiries window. Next to* FRANZ *is a middle-aged woman,* LILY.)

FRANZ: Am I in the right place?

LILY: They like you to wait.

> (*The trap suddenly goes up and a* CLERK *rings a bell. The first person in the queue goes up to the window.*)

> (*To* FRANZ) He's slipped up. You never want to be first. You're better off in the middle. Try and be routine. (*Pause.*) I don't even wear my glasses. You don't want a face anybody remembers. These are my documents.

> (*She is holding a folder.*)

> I crocheted the cover myself. I shall be all right today.

> (*Indicating the* OFFICIAL *at the window*) My friend's on. He's very refined, I've seen him in a café. There's the Tribunal.

> (*While* LILY *is talking,* THREE DISTINGUISHED FIGURES *pass through the hall.*)

> That coat's cashmere.

CLERK: Next.

> (LILY *is so absorbed in watching the* TRIBUNAL *arrive, she doesn't hear.*)

> Next.

> (FRANZ *nudges her and she rushes to the window and hands in her folder. Most of the following sequence is seen through the inquiries window. The* CLERK *opens Lily's folder and goes through her papers.*)

> Don't want to see that. Don't want to see that. I've seen that. Well? Nothing else?

> (LILY *says nothing. The* CLERK *thrusts the folder at her, and it falls on the floor.*)

> Next.

> (*As* FRANZ *steps up to the window,* LILY *is at his feet, gathering up her documents.*)

LILY: (*Looking up apologetically*) He's got mistaken. He's

confusing me with someone else.

(*The* CLERK *studies* FRANZ's *paper, clips a docket to it, makes a note, all the while carrying on a conversation with an unseen* OFFICIAL *behind him.*)

CLERK: Why Vienna?

OFFICIAL: I fancied a change.

CLERK: Don't we all?

INT. INQUIRIES OFFICE. DAY

We cut to inside the inquiries office. The CLERK *shows Franz's paper to the* OFFICIAL. *The* OFFICIAL *sits on a chair which is on castors, which enables him to slide down his desk towards the clerk.*

OFFICIAL: Dustbin job.

CLERK: Quite, but which one? The fourth-floor dustbin or the second-floor dustbin?

OFFICIAL: Who are we not friends with?

CLERK: 404?

OFFICIAL: 404. Anyway, they're supposed to like work, Jews.

(*The* CLERK *stamps the docket and hands it back to* FRANZ *through the window. We see* LILY *and* FRANZ *through the inquiries window.*)

LILY: (*Looking at Franz's docket*) That's this way.

INT. MAIN HALL/CORRIDOR TO LIFT, OFFICE BLOCK. DAY

FRANZ *leaves with his paper and docket, and follows* LILY *upstairs into a corridor.*

LILY: (*To* FRANZ) Come along. (*To* PASSERS-BY) Good morning.

(FRANZ *follows* LILY *into a lift. She nods to everybody, but particularly to* OFFICIALS, *though they do not respond.*)

INT. LIFT/CORRIDOR, OFFICE BLOCK. DAY

The gates of the lift clash to.

LILY: Good morning.

(*The* MAN *operating the gates has a gloved hand and works the gates with such abandon he could well have lost the other in the operation. The shot should emphasize the machinery of the gates, and any item (like scissors) we happen to see that is capable of*

93

inflicting an injury. There should also be an impression as the lift goes up of a large building, so that we hear the sounds from the various floors as the cage slowly ascends. In the lift is a young girl, a SEAMSTRESS, *with her hand bandaged. The* SEAMSTRESS *is talking to her neighbour in a low voice.*)

SEAMSTRESS: They said was I sleepy. I wasn't sleepy. I don't get sleepy. Lift and push, lift and push. How can you get sleepy? It's a skilled job. Then they made out the safety guard wasn't in position. It was in position, only I've got little hands. The guard is meant for a man's hands. (*Shows her bandaged hand and her whole hand to her neighbour.*) The spindles go in and out, in and out, stitching the pattern into the cloth. So naturally it stitched me to the cloth.

(LILY *and* FRANZ *come out of the lift*)

LILY: Good morning.

(FRANZ *follows* LILY *through a door and into a corridor. It is lofty with various doors off it and could be a corridor in an art gallery or a concert hall. Once through one of the doors the atmosphere is more muddled and intimate. The topography of the offices in general is intricate and illogical, rooms oddly located, sudden staircases, like the topography of a dream. The topography of* The Trial *is that of a dream (and not a nightmare particularly) and the office should be similar, though without losing touch with reality.* FRANZ *fails to close the door he and* LILY *have come through.*)

ATTENDANT: Door! Door! Door!

(FRANZ *walks up to the* ATTENDANT *and shows him his docket. He indicates for them to sit in the waiting area. Behind the* ATTENDANT *is a corridor lined with offices, partitioned off from the corridor and each other by a wall. The upper part of the wall is glass, divided into panes, like the partitions in nineteenth-century schools. It is therefore possible to see from the corridor into the offices and from one office into the next. The glass dividing screens have small sliding panels through which one office can communicate with the other, another odd dream-like feature.*)

INT. OFFICE AREA. DAY
In the office are three clerks, GUTLING, CULICK *and*

POHLMANN. GUTLING *is a large, fastidious creature,* CULICK *a bit of a Romeo and* POHLMANN *placid and plump. We see an* OFFICE GIRL *go through into Pohlmann's office with a cigar box.* POHLMANN *is interviewing a* WORKMAN.

POHLMANN: Now it's possible that your firm will try to put the blame on you.

(*The* WORKMAN *holds up his bandaged limb.*)

WORKMAN: Me?

POHLMANN: Yes. Just because you're the injured party, it doesn't mean you are not the guilty party.

(*Very low under the following* POHLMANN *dialogue, we hear* GUTLING *and the* JAM WORKMAN *in the next office.*)

GUTLING: (*Out of vision*) I can't find the form, of course, but we're assuming your employer is up to date with the premium. If he isn't I'm wasting your time and what's more important you're wasting mine. It says here you were scalded. What with?

JAM WORKMAN: (*Out of vision*) Jam.

GUTLING: (*Out of vision*) Jam?

The GUTLING *dialogue now becomes predominant.*

JAM WORKMAN: (*Out of vision*) Jam. You have to understand, sir, jam is not like water. It's syrup. It sticks.

GUTLING: (*Out of vision*) I know jam.

POHLMANN: (*Seeing the* GIRL *with the cigar box, in mock despair*) Oh no, not me. You haven't seen me. I'm not here.

(*The* COLLECTING GIRL *waits.*)

COLLECTING GIRL: Your grade are putting in five.

POHLMANN: My grade.

(*He puts a peeled boiled egg in his mouth, whole.*)

(POHLMANN *groans and puts a note in the box. The* COLLECTING GIRL *goes, and we go with her as we hear* POHLMANN *continuing with the questionnaire. Faded down under* GUTLING's *conversation.*)

Now, degree of incapacity.

95

(*We go with the* COLLECTING GIRL *as she goes along the corridor to the next-door room, but pauses with her hand on the handle of the door of* GUTLING'S *office as she sees another* GIRL *coming down the corridor. They chat, and we see beyond them into* GUTLING'S *office. A middle-aged* MAN *is telling* GUTLING *the story we have already half heard. The following conversations take place simultaneously.*)

JAM WORKMAN: I have two vats. The foreman said, 'I'm going to give you two vats. Normally it would be one, but I'm going to give *you* two.'

GUTLING: How long is the scar? (*He takes out a ruler*)

COLLECTING GIRL: I don't know whether I'm coming or going this morning. When are they going to have a whip round for me, that's what I want to know? Is your hair different?

FRIEND: I washed it.

COLLECTING GIRL: No. It looks different.

FRIEND: You're just not . . .

(*The* COLLECTING GIRL *is still poised, her hand on the door knob chatting. This annoys* GUTLING *who keeps glancing at her. Suddenly he jumps up, runs across the room and wrenches open the door.*)

GUTLING: Do you want me or not? Some of us are trying to work.

(*The* JAM WORKMAN *looks round at the* COLLECTING GIRL *and we see his scar.*)

COLLECTING GIRL: Everybody's putting in. It's for the Director.

GUTLING: How much?

COLLECTING GIRL: It's optional.

GUTLING: Rubbish.

COLLECTING GIRL: Five marks.

GUTLING: Here's four. I'm not like these other fellows. I have to look after my money.

(*The* JAM WORKMAN *has got up and is looking at the* COLLECTING GIRL.)

JAM WORKMAN: Excuse me, but aren't you a friend of my daughter?

96

COLLECTING GIRL: No.

JAM WORKMAN: Didn't she invite you to go on a cycling holiday in the mountains?

COLLECTING GIRL: No.

JAM WORKMAN: So the name Rosa means nothing to you?

(*The* COLLECTING GIRL *shakes her head.*)

GUTLING: It seems rude to interrupt but we appear to be losing sight of the job in hand . . .

(GUTLING *guides the* JAM WORKMAN *back into the room and we follow the* COLLECTING GIRL *down the corridor into the next office. In the next office* CULICK, *the youngest and best-looking of the clerks, is filling out a form. A* MAN *with his head bandaged sits by the desk.*)

GUTLING: (*Out of vision*)
 . . . Are you interested in compensation or aren't you?

CULICK: (*Shakes his head.*)
Your employer pays. The government pays.

HEAD-BANDAGED MAN: The shop said they are not responsible.

CULICK: (*Still writing*) Well, they normally do. (*Pause.*) What did you do with the ear? Did you save it.

HEAD-BANDAGED MAN: No.

CULICK: It's not important.

(*The* COLLECTING GIRL *has come in.* CULICK *gets up to talk to her.*)

You realize you're taking a risk, being alone in a room with me?

(*The* COLLECTING GIRL *is only slightly embarrassed and looks at the* HEAD-BANDAGED MAN.)

Women can't keep their hands off me, do you know that?

COLLECTING GIRL: It's only a gesture.

(*A* MAN *in a dust coat enters. He looks enquiringly round the office, spots an artificial leg leaning in a corner and goes and gets it.* CULICK *squeezes the* COLLECTING GIRL'*s breasts.*)

CULICK: So's that.

COLLECTING GIRL: Not now.

(CULICK *going back to talk to the* WORKMAN.)

CULICK: Does it incommode you in any way? Only having one ear? Do you wear glasses?

(*We follow the* MAN *in the dust coat as he leaves, and pick up* GUTLING *showing the* JAM WORKMAN *out, fading up their conversation.*)

GUTLING: . . . Can you or can you not lead a normal life? Since it's perfectly apparent that you can, I advise you to go away and lead it.

(*The* HEAD OF DEPARTMENT, *just arriving for work, comes along the corridor. He is with the* HEAD CLERK.)

HEAD OF DEPARTMENT: I was at the opera last night and it occurred to me . . .

GUTLING: Good morning, Head of Department.

(*The* HEAD OF DEPARTMENT *ignores him.*)

HEAD OF DEPARTMENT: The motor car.

HEAD CLERK: Head of Department?

HEAD OF DEPARTMENT: Potentially a significant accident statistic or not?

HEAD CLERK: No is my instinctive answer. Still, I'll give it some thought.

HEAD OF DEPARTMENT: Do.

(*They stop. The* HEAD CLERK *now withdraws.*)

HEAD CLERK: (*As he goes*) Oh, and Head of Department. Congratulations.

(*The* HEAD OF DEPARTMENT *nods complacently and departs as we follow the* HEAD CLERK *to Kafka's office. He opens the door and puts his head round.* KAFKA *is staring out of the window dictating to his secretary,* MISS WEBER, *who is taking it down in shorthand.*)

(*Mouthing at* MISS WEBER) Busy? Come back later.

(*He withdraws and by the time* KAFKA *has turned from the window he has gone.*)

KAFKA: (*Faded up*) . . . Although an extremely cautious operator would take care not to allow any joint of his fingers to project from the timber, the hand of even the most careful operator was bound to be drawn into the cutter space if it slipped. In such accidents usually several joints and even whole fingers were severed. Amen.

(*During the above,* KAFKA *has taken up a letter he has opened.*)

My brother-in-law tells me he's starting a factory. Can I help

him? (*Glances at* MISS WEBER.) Ear-rings today.
(*She fingers them.*)
Do they go right through?
(*She smiles and nods.*)
You had a hole dug in your ears! What courage!

MISS WEBER: It's my body.
(*Cut to the waiting area where* FRANZ *is sitting in line with* LILY. LILY *nudges* FRANZ *and indicates* KAFKA, *who has come down the corridor.*)

LILY: This is the fellow you want to see.
(FRANZ *rises and goes towards* GUTLING *and* KAFKA *who are talking to a* BUTCHER BOY *with a bandaged arm.* GUTLING *has taken the boy's folder and is studying it.*)

KAFKA: You've been in the wars.

BOY: Yes, sir.

GUTLING: (*Consulting the folder*) Our old friend the mincing machine. (*Reads the account of the accident.*) You stupid fool, putting your arm down.

BOY: The throat was too long. The truncheon wouldn't reach. You have to put your arm down.

KAFKA: Wasn't there a guard on the worm?

BOY: I took it off, sir.

GUTLING: Well, then it serves you right, then, doesn't it? In any case you don't belong here. You should be downstairs in 272.

BOY: I've just come from there.

KAFKA: Go back, and if they try and send you somewhere else say Doctor Kafka says to say you're not a football.
(*This is the first time we hear* KAFKA'*s name.*)

BOY: Yes, sir.

GUTLING: (*As they walk back down the corridor*) So, having fed himself into his machine, we now feed him into ours. Ha!
(FRANZ *follows them down the corridor trying to attract* KAFKA'*s attention.*)

FRANZ: Sir.
(*The* ATTENDANT *pulls him back and* KAFKA *ignores him with a smile.*)

KAFKA: Have you noticed how often when claimants are telling you about their accidents, they smile? Why do they smile?

They're apologizing. They feel foolish. Utterly blameless yet they feel guilty.

(GUTLING *goes into his office and we go with* KAFKA *into his, where the* HEAD CLERK *is looking at a report on Kafka's desk.*)

HEAD CLERK: Bricks falling on someone's head. Do they ever do anything else? I say, do they ever do anything else?

(KAFKA *moves over towards his desk.*)

KAFKA: Yet another firm trying to make out the fact they had an accident was sheer accident. Accidents, as we well know, are never an accident.

(*He sits. The* HEAD CLERK *peeps into the next office through the partition and finds* CULICK *staring into space, with* GUTLING *and* POHLMANN *beyond him, eavesdropping. The* HEAD CLERK *opens the panel in the partition.*)

HEAD CLERK: Get on. Get on. (CULICK *jumps to it but now it is* KAFKA *who is staring into space.*)

KAFKA: I thought of Japan.

(*The* HEAD CLERK *looks askance.*)

Bricks don't fall on people there. They have paper houses.

HEAD CLERK: They do, they do. Doctor Kafka . . .

KAFKA: Why is everything so heavy? This chair. This desk. The poor floor, carrying the burden. The sheer weight of Prague.

HEAD CLERK: Doctor Kafka. It's no secret we're losing our Head of Department. Elevated to the fifth floor. Higher things. A chance for a modest celebration. A presentation. A speech perhaps?

KAFKA: Excuse me, Head Clerk, but you have a small smut on your chin. Don't be alarmed.

(KAFKA *rubs the* HEAD CLERK's *chin with his handkerchief.*)

HEAD CLERK: Well?

KAFKA: Help! I must go and put my head under a circular saw.

INT. SAWMILL. DAY

A large sawmill with lots of overhead belts. It is a dangerous and tricky looking place and there is a dreadful din. The MANAGER *shows* KAFKA *a large circular saw.* KAFKA *examines the guard rails and looks under it, discussing it with the* MANAGER, *though all this is unheard through the din. Then* KAFKA *goes to another machine some*

distance away. This has no guard rail. A WORKMAN *is standing by,
watching. We see* KAFKA *turn to the* MANAGER *and point this out,
and ask him why, again unheard through the din. Mix through to:*

INT. OFFICE AREA. DAY
FRANZ *is still waiting, though now he sits by Pohlmann's desk.*
POHLMANN *and* GUTLING *are stood in front of an open filing
cabinet. Both are searching through the files.* POHLMANN *is eating a
sandwich as well as looking up the docket. He places the sandwich on
top of the open drawer.* CULICK *is standing next to* FRANZ *with his
foot on the desk – he is mending his shoe with glue.*

CULICK: Is it my imagination or do we get more shit than
　　anybody else?
GUTLING: Of course. There are four hundred people working in
　　this company. Since only two of them are Jews and one of
　　them happens to be Doctor Kafka we get sent a lot of shit.
　　It's only natural.
　　(POHLMANN *looks askance and then walks away from the
　　filing cabinet and, leaving his sandwich there, goes back to his
　　desk where* FRANZ *is sitting opposite.* GUTLING *removes the
　　sandwich from the file with an expression of distaste and puts it
　　on Pohlmann's desk.*)
POHLMANN: I don't seem to be able to trace it. When did you
　　have this accident?
FRANZ: It wasn't exactly an accident.
POHLMANN: Ah.
FRANZ: I'm ill through work.
CULICK: (*Still mending his shoes*) Well, I'm ill through work.
　　We're all ill through that.
　　(GUTLING, *having found what he was looking for, sits down on
　　the desk – on some paper which* CULICK *has been wiping his
　　glue on.*)
FRANZ: My skin's broken out. Look . . .
POHLMANN: (*Hastily*) No. We deal in accidents. You haven't
　　had an accident.
FRANZ: I get splashed with the dye. That's an accident, it
　　happens all the time.
GUTLING: So it's not an accident, is it?

(*He goes back to his desk where his* CLIENT *is waiting, the glued paper stuck to his trousers.*)

FRANZ: But it's fetched my skin out.

(*We cut to* GUTLING *returning to his office.*)

GUTLING: Look. This number here means that your firm has a policy that covers factory premises. It isn't a comprehensive cover for the firm's employees outside those premises.

(CULICK *enters.*)

CULICK: He doesn't want a rundown on the filing system.

(CULICK *has put his foot up on Gutling's desk and taken Gutling's scissors to cut off some fraying strands from the bottom of his trousers.*)

GUTLING: Why don't you put your foot on your own desk?

CULICK: Because I haven't any scissors.

(*The lunchtime bell rings.*)

Lunchtime!

GUTLING: (*Getting up*) I'm going to have to refer you back.

CLIENT: It was their barrel.

GUTLING: You're not our pigeon.

(CULICK *goes.*)

CLIENT: (*Who is limping*) And I ruined a perfectly good umbrella.

(*We follow him as he goes and end on* POHLMANN *and* FRANZ *in Pohlmann's office.*)

POHLMANN: It may clear up.

FRANZ: It's spreading all the time. Somebody said I should see Doctor Kafka. If he's a doctor he might know.

POHLMANN: Ah! He's not that sort of doctor.

FRANZ: It must be the dye. What else could it be? I've just got engaged to be married.

(POHLMANN *takes the folder and goes in search of* KAFKA, *but his office is empty.* MISS WEBER *comes in.*)

MISS WEBER: Whatever it is, the answer's no. Anyway he's gone to look at a sawmill. (*Takes the papers and glances at them.*) No. No. You should know better than this.

(*She starts to touch him up, rubbing her hand over his thigh.*)

POHLMANN: It's a borderline case. He may be interested.

MISS WEBER: Don't be ridiculous. Of course he'd be interested.

He's got enough on his plate.

(POHLMANN *and* MISS WEBER *are seen from* FRANZ's *point of view through the glass partitions.*)

He remarked on my new ear-rings. You haven't.

(POHLMANN *grasps her breasts.*)

POHLMANN: What lovely ear-rings.

(*As* POHLMANN *kisses* MISS WEBER *he slips the folder on to Kafka's desk. A telephone rings and* MISS WEBER *goes to answer it. Cut back to Pohlmann's office and* FRANZ *who has been watching them kissing.* POHLMANN *returns.*)

I've put it on his desk. Come back tomorrow.

FRANZ: What I want is an independent medical examination. By a specialist. It must be the dye.

POHLMANN: I've put it on his desk.

FRANZ: I just got engaged.

POHLMANN: So you keep telling me. Come tomorrow.

(FRANZ *goes.* LILY *is waiting for him and they go together.*)

INT. GYMNASIUM. NIGHT

FRANZ (YOUNG) *exercising at night on the rings in the moonlight.*

FRANZ (OLD): (*Voice over*) I'd started going to the gym at night. I didn't want anybody to see my skin. At the Institute where I did want somebody to see my skin, nobody would look. I went again and waited.

(*Mix through to:*)

INT. OFFICE AREA. DAY

PETITIONERS *waiting, including* FRANZ *and* LILY.

LILY: (*Looking straight ahead*) Do you hear that? Because I can hear a river. I never used to be able to hear a river. They say, 'Well, a river's nice to hear.' Not in your own head it isn't. The first thing I'm going to get is some new chair covers. Delayed concussion.

(POHLMANN *and* CULICK *are already in their offices, when* GUTLING *storms in, in a towering rage. He wrenches open the glass partition between his and Culick's office.*)

GUTLING: How long have I been in this department?

CULICK: I thought it was five years.

GUTLING: I thought it was five years, but it can't be. Because when the Head Clerk wants someone to make a presentation to the Director does he ask me? No, he doesn't. He asks Doctor Kafka who's only been here one year. So maybe I haven't been here five years. Maybe it only seems like five years. Maybe I only came here yesterday. Maybe I don't work here at all. Well, we'll see about that. Because I am now going to start making my presence felt.

(*He goes out of the office down the line of waiting* CLAIMANTS.)

Docket. Show me. Come on. Docket. Docket. Docket. (*Examines one.*) Well, you don't belong here for a start.

CLAIMANT: I was told . . .

GUTLING: You mustn't believe what you're told. Not in this place. I was told this was going to be a job with prospects. I don't care what you were told. This is a P48. It is not our pigeon. Out. Out. Out. Out. (*To* CLAIMANTS *in turn*) You've no business here either. Out. Out.

(*Then it is* FRANZ's *turn.*)

Out.

FRANZ: I'm supposed to see Doctor Kafka.

GUTLING: Doctor Kafka is a busy man. Doctor Kafka has factories to inspect. Doctor Kafka has a speech to prepare. Out. Out. Out. Out. Out.

(GUTLING *pushes* FRANZ *and the others out.*)

INT. LIFT. DAY

KAFKA's *calm face coming up in the lift.*

GUTLING: (*Voice over, screaming*) Out. Out. Out. (*many times*).

(*Cut to high shot of the lift coming up.*)

INT. OFFICE AREA. DAY

Cut back to GUTLING *expelling the rest of the* CLAIMANTS.

GUTLING: Back, madam, back to where you came from. Out. Out. Out. Out!

(*He shoves the last of the* CLAIMANTS *out and turns to face the audience of* CLERKS *and* SECRETARIES *who have come out of their offices to watch his mad behaviour. Nervously they go back to work as* GUTLING *barges through them to his office.*)

INT. CORRIDOR/STAIRS OUTSIDE ROOM 404. DAY
KAFKA *walking towards the office, puzzled by the stream of*
CLAIMANTS *leaving.*

INT. OFFICE AREA. DAY
MISS WEBER, *in the process of handing out coffee to the* CLERKS,
walks down the corridor between offices and meets KAFKA.
MISS WEBER: Someone's on the war path.
    (KAFKA *sees* GUTLING *fuming at his desk and approaches.*)
KAFKA: Charles.
    (GUTLING *rises to meet* KAFKA *at the doorway.*)
    I want to see this young man. He's a dyeworker. Some sort of
    eczema.
    (*He has been looking in a folder.*)
GUTLING: Gone. I've just sent him away.
KAFKA: Ah.
GUTLING: He wasn't our responsibility.
KAFKA: I'm sure you're right. You're always right.
    Incidentally . . .
    (KAFKA *draws* GUTLING *aside. They move off down the
    corridor.*) I've been landed with a speech of farewell to the
    Head of Department, I was wondering . . . could you give
    me a pointer or two?
    (*It is an exercise in pure charm. They stop.*)
GUTLING: Happy to.
KAFKA: How's mother?
GUTLING: She's well. Very well.
KAFKA: (*Going*) Good. Good. About this dyeworker. Can
    you . . . retrieve him?
GUTLING: Ah!
    (*He is nonplussed but* CULICK, *coming out of his office, saves*
    GUTLING's *face.*)
CULICK: I think I fancy a bit of a promenade myself.

INT. MAIN HALL, OUTSIDE INQUIRIES OFFICE. DAY
The INQUIRIES CLERK *stamps Franz's docket.* FRANZ *now
has another piece of paper clipped to his growing sheaf of
documents.*

INQUIRIES CLERK: 452 . . . next!

>(FRANZ *is walking across the large hall, when a* MAN *runs down the steps and through the hall.*)

MAN: (*Shouting*) I've got it. I've got my claim. I've got it. I've got my claim. I've got it. I've got it. I've got it . . . My claim . . . I've got it, I've got it, I've got it. I've got my claim. I've got it.

>(FRANZ *shows his docket to an* ATTENDANT.)

ATTENDANT: 452!

>(FRANZ *moves off.*)

INT. CORRIDOR. DAY

FRANZ *walks away from a stairwell and along a corridor. He passes a gents lavatory and goes in. We hold on the corridor as* CULICK *rounds the corner and strides straight past the gents.*

INT. TALL WOMAN'S OFFICE/CORRIDOR. DAY

A TALL WOMAN *stands in front of a mirror. She sees how she looks with a bundle of assorted documents. She is still gauging the effect of this when* CULICK *comes in.*

TALL WOMAN: (*Still looking at herself*) To what do we owe this pleasure?

CULICK: We've lost a claimant. Inquiries said they'd sent him up here.

TALL WOMAN: I haven't seen him (*Turns towards him.*) You're talking to someone who's just received a summons to the fifth floor.

>(*They go out into the corridor and she locks the door.*)

CULICK: If he surfaces, point him back upstairs, would you? I'll do the same for you sometime.

TALL WOMAN: Can I have that in writing?

>(*The* TALL WOMAN *and* CULICK *go along the corridor and exit. The corridor is empty for a second then a* CHILD *with a broom much too large for it comes out of a door and plays at sweeping.* FRANZ *coming along the corridor sees the* CHILD *just as the door opens and a hand pulls the* CHILD *inside again. The* CHILD *screams 'Ow'. We hear a slap.* FRANZ *tries the door of the Tall Woman's office (452). It is locked.* FRANZ *now begins*

to wander about the Workers Accident Insurance Building.)

INT. CORRIDOR/WAITING ROOM. DAY
FRANZ *walks down a wide corridor, through some strange wooden barriers, towards the Tribunal waiting room.*

ONE-LEGGED MAN: (*Voice over*) They were very pleased with me at the hospital. The doctor said, 'You got that fast in the loom?' He said, 'Well, you're lucky.' He said, 'If I'd had to take it off in the theatre I couldn't have done it cleaner than that.' And he said, 'You're fortunate in another respect'; I said, 'Yes?' He said, 'You're an extrovert.' He said, 'You've got the right attitude of mind.' I said, 'I have. It's a bit unsightly, but I'm not incommoded. In some respects the reverse. More room in the bed; more scope for manoeuvre. I haven't noticed the wife complaining. (*Laughs.*) Mind you it's a wonder I didn't lose more than a leg. I pointed out there was no cradle on the shaft. After I'd had my accident I said to the foreman, 'You haven't got a leg to stand on.' He said. 'You can talk.'
(*By now,* FRANZ *has come upon a long line of people sitting waiting outside a pair of double doors. A uniformed* ATTENDANT *guards the doors. We now see the* ONE-LEGGED MAN *whose voice we've been hearing.*)
He said, 'They'll claim you were drunk.' I said, 'Drunk? Pull the other one.' He said 'What other one?' I said 'Precisely.' (*Guffaws.*) You have to laugh. Anyway, last lap.

MAN WITHOUT EAR: End in sight.

ONE-LEGGED MAN: Where will you go tomorrow? Eh? Where will you go? Won't know you're born.

MAN WITHOUT EAR: It's a way of life. (*Addressing the* ATTENDANT) You're used to it, people coming and going. It's our big day.

ATTENDANT: Keep it down, keep it down.
(FRANZ *sits down next to the* ONE-LEGGED MAN)

ONE-LEGGED MAN: Here you are. Sit this side. More leg room. Ha ha. (*Takes* FRANZ's *dockets and looks at them.*) I say. This brings back memories.
(*Shows it to* MAN WITHOUT EAR.)

MAN WITHOUT EAR: Eh?

ONE-LEGGED MAN: I say, 'This brings back memories.'

MAN WITHOUT EAR: Oh my goodness me!

FRANZ: I'm wanting a certificate to see the doctor.

MAN WITHOUT EAR: What doctor?

FRANZ: Their doctor.

ONE-LEGGED MAN: You haven't seen the doctor? Hey. He hasn't even seen the doctor!

MAN WITHOUT EAR: He hasn't seen the doctor.

(This information passes down the line and FRANZ *becomes an object of scrutiny. They should be reminiscent of characters in* Alice in Wonderland.)

ATTENDANT: Keep it down. Keep it down.

ONE-LEGGED MAN: How long have you been coming?

FRANZ: Today.

ONE-LEGGED MAN: This is your first day? Listen, it's taken me six months to get this far.

BALD MAN: *(Taking off his wig and rubbing his totally bald head)* It's taken me a year.

FRANZ: Not every day?

MAIMED WOMAN: All I want is to be a normal person.

ATTENDANT: Keep it down. Keep it down.

ONE-LEGGED MAN: I went three months and never heard a thing.

MAN WITHOUT EAR: You haven't assembled any documents. You've got to assemble documents.

FRANZ: I just want to see the doctor.

ONE-LEGGED MAN: Well, this isn't the doctor. This is the Tribunal. It's the Panel is this. You don't belong here.

FRANZ: What should I do?

ONE-LEGGED MAN: Don't ask me. We don't want them upsetting. You've no business here. Now clear off. Go on, clear off. We want it all plain sailing. Bugger off. Go on.

MAN WITHOUT EAR: *(Simultaneous with above)* Go on. Go on, get out.

(Their attention is distracted by the door opening. A CLAIMANT *comes out. Sudden silence.)*

ATTENDANT: Next.
> (*A* GIRL *goes into the room while the others question the* CLAIMANT *who has just come out.*)

MAIMED WOMAN: Well?

CLAIMANT: I made a good impression.

MAIMED WOMAN: How many are there?

CLAIMANT: Three. One doesn't speak. Just looks.

MAIMED WOMAN: Looks?

CLAIMANT: I was missing my birth certificate. One of them said could I give them my word that I had been born.
> (*The others laugh.*)

They all laughed.

MAIMED WOMAN: Laughed?

CLAIMANT: They said now to try and lead a normal life.

ATTENDANT: All right, all right.
> (*He ushers the* CLAIMANT *out.* MAN WITHOUT EAR *shakes his head.*)

MAN WITHOUT EAR: Disallowed. They always tell you. In the last stage, they always tell you.

ATTENDANT: Now make sure you've all got your documents. And that they're in the right order.
> (*They all look through them like* Alice *characters.* FRANZ *goes up to the* ATTENDANT *to show him his docket. The* ATTENDANT *waves it away.*)

Are you on this list? Not interested. Not interested. List only. Out! (*He pushes* FRANZ *out.*)

INT. UPSTAIRS CORRIDOR/ROOM. DAY
FRANZ *comes along another upstairs corridor, less grand, more attic-like than the other.* LILY *is sitting on a chair outside a door.*

LILY: Where do you want? (*Looks at* FRANZ's *docket.*) They'll take that in here, yes. My documents have just gone in. They're studying them now, possibly.
> (*A* GIRL *comes along the corridor carrying a mug and a comb.*)

Hello, Teresa.
> (*The* GIRL *ignores her.*)

Their dog's poorly. She's got a lot on her mind.

(FRANZ *is increasingly dubious of this woman.*)

FRANZ: I'm not sure I shouldn't tell them I'm here.

LILY: No. You'll go to the bottom of the pile. (*Pause.*) The girl
said last week my file was taken out by the Assistant Manager.
Of course I know them all here, I'm like one of the family.

(*Another* GIRL *passes.*)

Sheila . . .

(*To* FRANZ) Sheila. I'd liked to have worked in a place like
this. A sedentary occupation but with some coming and
going. Banter. Whip-rounds. Relations between the sexes.
Sat at home, it's no game, is it?

(FRANZ *listens at the door. She gets agitated.*)

Come away. They're just digesting the facts.

FRANZ: Get off.

LILY: No, you're young. You don't understand.

FRANZ: Look. I could be stuck here all day.

(*He pushes* LILY *back into the chair quite violently. He knocks
on the door. Quietly. Then louder. He opens the door. There is a
broom. A bucket and some newspapers on the floor.*)

There's nobody here. Come and see.

LILY: No. I'll wait till I'm called.

FRANZ: There's nobody there. Look.

(*He drags her towards door.*)

LILY: Don't shout. There's offices everywhere. Leave off. I'm a
woman. I've had a head injury.

FRANZ: It's an empty room.

(*He pushes her into it violently.*)

LILY: Stop it.

FRANZ: It's empty.

LILY: (*Simultaneously with the above*) You've just got to
be . . . patient.

FRANZ: Look at it.

LILY: (*On her hands and knees*) You've no business . . .

FRANZ: . . . empty!

LILY: (*Picking up the old newspapers*) Look, these are important.

FRANZ: They're not important. They're rubbish.

(FRANZ *hits her with some newspaper.*)

LILY: That's wicked, wicked. You're not supposed to hit
    women, everybody says.
    (FRANZ *runs up the steps leading up out of the room.*)
FRANZ: You're mad. You're wrong in the head.
    (*He throws some papers on to her head.*)
LILY: These are important – these are to do with my case.
FRANZ: You're mad.
LILY: You're young. You don't know.
    (FRANZ *is running up a winding staircase littered with papers.*
    We see LILY *far below him. He then runs along a high, narrow*
    corridor.)
    (*Voice over*) Papers, facts, they all come into it, possibly.
    You've got to keep track. You . . . you don't understand.

INT. SMALL HALL/BALCONY. DAY
FRANZ *climbs a poky staircase, which we see from above as if it is a*
vortex. He comes through a door and on to the balcony of a hall, like a
small concert hall where the Tribunal is sitting. Three MEN *are sitting*
behind a table on a platform. Standing before them is a GIRL *naked.*
THIN DOCTOR: (*Reading out a report*) . . . breaking the left arm
    and causing widespread abrasions to the chest and abdomen
    the scars from which you can plainly see.
ANGRY DOCTOR: Well, not all that plainly, surely?
THIN DOCTOR: Quite plainly. Look. Raise your arms again. Yes.
FAT DOCTOR: Yes.
THIN DOCTOR: (*Sweetly*) Go on, shall I? She reports some loss of
    feeling on her left side.
ANGRY DOCTOR: 'Course she does. She's not stupid. Some dozy
    general practitioner has probably said to her, 'Do you have
    any loss of feeling on your left side?' and lo and behold she
    suddenly finds she's got some loss of feeling on her left side.
THIN DOCTOR: (*Patiently*) Her doctor reports there to have been
    some personality change.
ANGRY DOCTOR: Probably the same doctor.
THIN DOCTOR: She is subject to violent changes of mood,
    incapable of sustained attention.
ANGRY DOCTOR: I don't believe any of this.
    (*There is a silence.*)

THIN DOCTOR: I beg your pardon?

ANGRY DOCTOR: Has it ever occurred to you that everyone who comes before this panel has, prior to their accident, been of a sunny and equable disposition, capable of long periods of sustained attention, unvisited by headaches or indeed any infirmity at all, the mind alert, the body in perfect order, a paragon of health. Take this young woman. Previously a cheerful soul, she is now said to be anxious and depressed. So? Previously an optimist she is now a pessimist, is that such a bad thing? One could say that this accident has brought her to her senses rather than deprived her of them. She now takes a dim view of the world. So do I. She can't keep her mind on the matter in hand. Nor can I. She winces when she looks in the mirror. So do I.

THIN DOCTOR: She's crying.

FAT DOCTOR: So am I.

ANGRY DOCTOR: We cannot compensate people for being cast out of Paradise. All these sheaves of reports are saying is 'I didn't know how lucky I was till this happened.' So? Now they do know. They have achieved wisdom. And a degree of self-knowledge. They should be paying us, not we them. We appear to have a visitor.

(*The* ANGRY DOCTOR *has spotted* FRANZ. *The* THIN DOCTOR *stands up, angry. The* WOMAN *covers herself up.*)

THIN DOCTOR: What are you doing here?

FRANZ: I want someone to tell me what's wrong with me.

THIN DOCTOR: You've no business here. This is outrageous.

(FAT DOCTOR *stands.*)

FAT DOCTOR: The idea.

THIN DOCTOR: Get out.

FRANZ: Not until somebody tells me where to go.

FAT DOCTOR: Call someone. Call the doorman.

THIN DOCTOR: Doorman!

(*The door springs open and the* ATTENDANT *rushes on to the balcony and seizes* FRANZ. *He drags him down to the Tribunal.*)

Mad. Mad. Mad, sir, mad.

(FRANZ *struggles with him.*)

ANGRY DOCTOR: (*To the* ATTENDANT) Stop it, you animal.

You're not in a farmyard.

ATTENDANT: Yes, sir. Thank you, sir.

ANGRY DOCTOR: Let me see that paper.

(FRANZ *gives him his docket.*)

(*To* FRANZ) Come with me. (*Rises.*) Any excuse to get away
from this collective idiocy. (*Shouts back at the panel.*) Idiocy.
Come along.

INT. WAITING ROOM OUTSIDE TRIBUNAL. DAY

FRANZ *follows the* ANGRY DOCTOR, *the* CLAIMANTS *are lined
up outside.*

ANGRY DOCTOR: I hope you're all word perfect on your
personality changes. (*Strides at great speed along the corridor,
talking to himself*) It's a wicked world. It's a wicked, wicked
world. I have lost my faith. Doctor loses faith. Doctor goes
way of other doctors.

(*He and* FRANZ *stop.*)

It just needs one person, just one to come before that panel
and say, 'Doctor, since suffering this grievous affliction I am
a new man, a better person.'

(*They move off.*)

'The loss of my hand has been an education. Blinded, I can
now see.' Instead of which it's 'How much is it worth?'

ONE-LEGGED MAN: Doctor!

(*The* ONE-LEGGED MAN *stands up, supported by his crutch.*)

ANGRY DOCTOR: How much do you think this is worth, eh?

(*He takes the crutch and hurls it down. Without the crutch the*
ONE-LEGGED MAN *falls over. The* ANGRY DOCTOR *turns to*
FRANZ.)

How much is whatever you've got worth? (*As they continue
walking*) I'm not a doctor any more. I'm an accountant.

INT. CORRIDOR OUTSIDE TALL WOMAN'S OFFICE. DAY

The ANGRY DOCTOR *and* FRANZ *arrive outside the Tall Woman's
office.*

ANGRY DOCTOR: This it? (*Looks at* FRANZ's *docket*) Yes.
Journey's end.

(*The door opens and the* TALL WOMAN *comes out.*)

TALL WOMAN: Ah! The lost sheep.

ANGRY DOCTOR: Blessed are the maimed for they shall be
    compensated.
    (*The* ANGRY DOCTOR *goes.*)

TALL WOMAN: Come on.
    (*She goes down the corridor and round the corner, followed by a
    confused* FRANZ.)

MISS WEBER: (*Voice over*) Don't you sometimes just long to see
    one . . .

INT. OFFICE AREA. DAY

POHLMANN *and* MISS WEBER *in Pohlmann's office.*

POHLMANN *eating as usual, sandwich in one hand, the other hand
on* MISS WEBER'*s bottom, though she betrays no sign of this on her
face except for a slight wavering in her voice.*

MISS WEBER: (*Reading from a file*) . . . single able-bodied
    person. Someone who doesn't lack an arm here or a finger
    there, who doesn't pull up their shirt without wanting to
    reveal some frightful burn. Somebody normal?
    (*The door opens and the* TALL WOMAN *shows* FRANZ *into the
    office.* POHLMANN *hurriedly removes his hand from* MISS
    WEBER.)

TALL WOMAN: Your lost sheep.
    (*She goes.*)

POHLMANN: Oh, take a seat.
    (FRANZ *doesn't.*)

FRANZ: I was here this morning . . . I've been all over. I was
    supposed to see Doctor Kafka.

MISS WEBER: Doctor Kafka has gone home. His hours are eight
    until two.

FRANZ: Does that mean I have to come back?

POHLMANN: You have reached the beginning. You are about to
    start. You have been allowed to enter the race.

FRANZ: Look. I'm covered in scale.
    (*He shows them his hands and a shower of scurf falls on the
    desk.*)

MISS WEBER: You're not. Your face is perfectly normal. Don't
    exaggerate.

POHLMANN: (*Filling in a form*) This gives you an appointment
      with the Institute doctor. They're having public clinics on
      Thursdays. He will look at you and decide if he thinks this
      skin complaint is anything to do with an accident at work.
FRANZ: I've told you. I haven't had an accident.
MISS WEBER: So why go on? Stop now. Before it's too late.
POHLMANN: No new process? No new chemicals? Nothing new
      in your life?
FRANZ: I've just got engaged.
MISS WEBER: (*Drily*) Any accident there?

INT. CHRISTINA'S PARENTS APARTMENT. NIGHT
FRANZ *and his fiancée,* CHRISTINA, *are sitting awkwardly in the
formal parlour. The* OLD LADY *in a wheelchair is there also.*
CHRISTINA *tries to kiss him.* FRANZ *looks unhappy, and indicates
the* OLD LADY *as an excuse.* CHRISTINA *rises, then turns the
wheelchair round so that the* OLD LADY *is facing the wall. She closes
the doors. She slowly unbuttons her dress to reveal her breasts.* FRANZ
looks away, tears in his eyes. CHRISTINA *turns away, angry.*

INT. RAILWAY STATION/PLATFORM, PRAGUE. DAY
*A steam train has just arrived at the platform. From the other side of
the train we see* FRANZ *standing looking at his* FATHER *who has just
got off a train. He is a peasant and is much smaller than* FRANZ. *He
embraces his son.*
FRANZ (OLD): (*Voice over*) I'd written to my father. He was
      a peasant. The family were in . . . well, it's now
      Germany . . . he came to Prague. I think of my father then
      as an old man. But he was younger than I am now. He had
      remedies of his own.

INT. STATION LAVATORY. DAY
FRANZ *and his* FATHER *are in a cubicle.* FRANZ *has his shirt open.
Franz's* FATHER *spreads out some kind of leaves, presses them to his
son's chest. We see* FRANZ'S *face. He is touched by his* FATHER'S
love but he has no faith in this remedy.

INT. FRANZ'S LODGINGS. NIGHT
FRANZ *is asleep. His* FATHER *is sitting in a chair by his bedside, his hat on. He takes it off.*

INT. MEDICAL SCHOOL ENTRANCE. DAY
KAFKA *rushing in, late, confronted by several staircases, and trying to find his way into the auditorium.*

LECTURER (SENIOR DOCTOR): (*Out of vision*) All in all it's a
    pretty mixed bag, but slanted on the whole in the direction of
    injury at work. Plus some teasers for the . . .

INT. AUDITORIUM, MEDICAL SCHOOL. DAY
Sitting at the back of the auditorium, Franz's FATHER *watches.*

LECTURER: . . . people in the fourth year and also some
    interesting examples of occupational disease. Increasing
    industrialization means this field of medicine is bound to
    expand. I imagine that's why many of you are here.
    (*Some laughter. We follow* KAFKA *in, to reveal the* SENIOR
    DOCTOR *standing before the auditorium full of* STUDENTS.
    KAFKA *sits down.*)
    Physical conditions, some of which you will see, take time to
    declare themselves and I would ask you to remember that we
    are seeing today casualties of conditions in the industry of
    twenty, even thirty years ago, conditions which . . .
    (*This speech continuing under, we cut to a group of* PATIENTS,
    *sitting on benches at the side of the auditorium all made ready in
    linen gowns. Among them, we note* LILY. *An* ATTENDANT *sits
    next to them.* FRANZ, *gowned, and ready, is sitting waiting.*)

MAN: I'm a miracle. I have a   LECTURER: (*Out of vision*)
    hole in my stomach. They   . . . in all likelihood have
    watch the food passing   since been improved.
    through.   Industrial safety is bound
YOUNG WOMAN: He's had an   to lag behind medical
    article written about him.   knowledge . . .
    Show him your article.

(*We now cut back to the* LECTURER)

LECTURER: . . . and doubtless in thirty or forty years' time
    when I hope I shall be safely tucked up in my grave . . .

(*We cut back to the* PATIENTS *as the speech goes on under.*)

(*The* MAN *begins to show his article to* FRANZ.)

YOUNG WOMAN: He's famous with doctors. Somebody came from Paris to see him. And they pay.

LECTURER: (*Out of vision*) . . . my hapless successor will still be stood here. Legislation is after all only a net.

ATTENDANT: Ssh!

(*Cut back to* LECTURER.)

LECTURER: Nowadays the mesh may be wide. But if you believe in progress, which I do not, the mesh will get smaller and the number of people suffering from industrial injury will dwindle. But it won't, of course: because there will be new industries and new industries mean new diseases. You have chosen a wise profession, gentlemen. Doctors will never be unemployed. Now could we have our first conundrum please.

(*The* ATTENDANT *signals to* FRANZ.)

ATTENDANT: Come on.

(FRANZ *walks on to the stage, watched by* KAFKA. FRANZ *is standing in a pool of light on the stage.*)

LECTURER: (*To* FRANZ) Disrobe.

(FRANZ *does so, and stands naked. We see his scaly chest, and as the* LECTURER *indicates for him to turn round, his back also.*)

(*To* STUDENTS) Well? (*Seeing* STUDENT *raise his hand.*) Yes.

FIRST STUDENT: Is it a form of psoriasis?

LECTURER: Wonderful. Anybody got any brilliant ideas about the aetiology? Patient is in no discomfort. Affected areas don't itch, not sore. Well, come on, come on. What sort of question should we be asking?

SECOND STUDENT: What age is the patient?

LECTURER: (*To* FRANZ) How old are you?

FRANZ: Twenty-six.

LECTURER: Twenty-six.

THIRD STUDENT: Married or single?

FRANZ: Single.

FOURTH STUDENT: Is it venereal in origin?
>   (*The* LECTURER *looks at* FRANZ, *whom he thinks has not*
>   *understood*.)
LECTURER: Did you get it from a tart?
FRANZ: (*Passionately*) No.
LECTURER: Patient says no. Patient probably right.
>   (FIFTH STUDENT *raises hand*.)
>   Well?
FIFTH STUDENT: Could it be nervous?
LECTURER: Are you asking me or are you asking the patient?
>   (*During the next section we see* KAFKA *watching intently*.)
>   We know what he does. He works in a dyeworks. But what
>   sort of a fellow is he . . . is he nervous, highly strung,
>   cheerful, not cheerful? Look, what are we supposed to be
>   doing here? Who are you? I thought you were supposed to be
>   medical students.
FRANZ: (*Shouting*) What is it? What have I done? Give me
>   something. Give me something for it. Stop it. It's all over my
>   body. Why? Why?
>   (*We see Franz's* FATHER, *tears running down his face. He leaves*.)

INT. MEDICAL SCHOOL ENTRANCE. DAY
We leave with Franz's FATHER. *He sits at the bottom of the ornate*
staircase in the entrance hall.
LECTURER: (*Voice over*) Gentlemen will note agitation of patient
>   and need to assess degree of proper agitation due to patient's
>   physical condition as distinct from evidence of neurotic
>   instability. Next patient, please.

INT. AUDITORIUM, MEDICAL SCHOOL
The LECTURER *standing on the stage*. LILY *is sitting beside him in a*
pool of light.
LECTURER: Some of you might say that there is nothing wrong
>   with the patient. Once upon a time she met with a slight
>   accident at work.

INT. MEDICAL SCHOOL ENTRANCE. DAY
FRANZ, *once more in his own clothes, comes down the steps to meet his*

FATHER. *They leave.*

LECTURER: (*Voice over*) A box fell on her head. She took a few days off and she felt none the worse. But then she heard that in this enlightened age there is compensation for those that suffer injury at work.

INT. AUDITORIUM, MEDICAL SCHOOL. DAY
THE LECTURER *and* LILY, *on the stage in the auditorium.*

LECTURER: 'Is she entitled to this?' she wonders. And the wondering turns to worrying as she begins to lie awake at night suffering from headaches. She is increasingly unhappy. (KAFKA *listens intently to this.*)
And so begins her quest for compensation but for what? Not the injury, for she has scarcely suffered one. And she is not malingering for the headaches are real. And to those of you who say there is no injury therefore there can be no compensation she can say, 'But I was not like this before my accident. I had no quest. Looking for what is wrong with me *is* what is wrong with me!'

INT. ENTRANCE TO RAILWAY STATION. DAY
FRANZ *is seeing his* FATHER *off. They embrace.* FRANZ, *weeping, runs off down the steps as his* FATHER *turns to go.*

INT. OFFICE AREA/CORRIDOR. DAY
A cake on a trolley is pushed along the corridor by two SECRETARIES. GUTLING *and* CULICK *and others follow it along the corridor. In Kafka's office, seen from the corridor,* KAFKA *is dressed up and is trying to tie his bow-tie.* POHLMANN *is sitting at his desk, working.* MISS WEBER *comes in with a bottle of wine and a plate of food.*

MISS WEBER: The good doctor didn't want you to feel left out.

POHLMANN: And the cigar?
    (MISS WEBER *goes.*)

INT. OFFICE. DAY
The party. KAFKA *is speaking. The room is crowded. The* HEAD OF DEPARTMENT *in the place of honour. We see Kafka's colleagues, the* HEAD CLERK, *all the staff.*

KAFKA: In my four districts people fall off the scaffolding as if they were drunk, or they fall into the machines, all the beams topple, all embankments give way, all ladders slide, whatever people carry up, falls down, whatever they hand down they stumble over.

(*Laughter through much of this from* GUTLING.)

And I have a headache . . .

INT. OFFICE AREA. DAY

During this speech, cut to the empty office area, where POHLMANN *is alone.* FRANZ *enters.*

KAFKA: (*Out of vision*) . . . from all those girls in porcelain factories who incessantly throw themselves down the stairs with mountains of dishware.

(*Hoots of laughter.*)

I say this only because in making this speech, I fully expect to fall on my face . . .

(*Fade down sound.*)

. . . and when I do, Herr Head of Department, please remember that it has been in the proper course of my duties and I shall expect to be compensated.

(*More laughter.*)

INT. POHLMANN'S OFFICE. DAY

POHLMANN *is working.* FRANZ *comes in slightly drunk.* KAFKA'*s speech continues under, but inaudible.*

FRANZ: Why do you work here? This is a terrible place. It's a place of torture.

POHLMANN: One has to do something.

(*He holds out his hand for* FRANZ'*s papers out of shot.*)

I need your papers for your file.

FRANZ: I don't want money. I want it to be given a name. How can I ever get rid of it if it doesn't have a name?

(*Suddenly he picks up the bottle of wine and flings it through a window.*)

INT. OFFICE. DAY

Cut back to KAFKA *speaking at the party. The sound of shattering glass is heard.*

KAFKA: *Voilà.* An accident.
(*More laughter.*)
Our thanks then to the benign ruler of our topsy-turvy
world. This kingdom of the absurd, where it does not pay to
be well, where loss determines gain, limbs become
commodities and to be given a clean bill of health is to be
sent away empty-handed. Our world, where to be deprived is
to be endowed, to be disfigured means to be marked out for
reward and to limp is to jump every hurdle. The Director
guards us, the workers of the Workers Accident Institute
against our own institutional accidents. And I don't mean
falling over the holes in the linoleum on the bottom corridor,
(Maintenance please note).
(*Laughter.*)

INT. OFFICE AREA. DAY
POHLMANN *sitting at his desk with* FRANZ *sitting opposite him. An*
OLD MAILMAN *trundles his carriage along the corridor and past the*
office.
KAFKA: (*Out of vision*) I mean blindness to genuine need,
deafness to a proper appeal and hardness of heart. These are
our particular professional risks for which there are no safety
guards, no grids, no protective clothing. Only a scrupulous
and vigilant humanity.

INT. OFFICE. DAY
Cut back to the party.
KAFKA: A toast then to the benevolent umpire in our absurd
games, our firm but kindly father to whom without fear we
can always turn, as we do now and say, Herr Director.
(*They toast him – 'Herr Director' – and people applaud.*)

INT. OFFICE AREA. DAY
The office staff are coming away from the party.
CULICK: He can certainly talk.
GUTLING: Or course he can talk. But I can talk. You haven't
heard me talk.
CULICK: Haven't I?

121

GUTLING: Not in a formal situation.

CULICK: Does that make a difference?

GUTLING: I'd have told him. I'd have used the opportunity to let them know exactly what's wrong with this place.

CULICK: Yes.

(*They disappear into their respective offices.* KAFKA *is in his room, still dressed up, when* POHLMANN *brings in* FRANZ. MISS WEBER *is filing away papers.*)

KAFKA: Yes?

POHLMANN: The dyeworker.

MISS WEBER: Not again. Really.

KAFKA: (*Fiercely*) Silence. (*Pause.*) Please. Sit down.

(FRANZ *does so.*)

FRANZ: I've been told you are kind. I've been told you are the one to see. They say you are a human being.

KAFKA: No, I do a very good imitation of a human being.

FRANZ: You are harder to see than anybody.

MISS WEBER: There has to be a procedure. A system. Is that so terrible?

KAFKA: What did you want to say to me?

MISS WEBER: There is nothing to say. It is a hopeless case. People coming in, wanting money.

FRANZ: I don't want money.

MISS WEBER: Nobody ever does. I sometimes wonder what they think they're doing here, it comes as such a shock. 'You mention money to me when I've lost my precious fingers.' 'All my treasured auburn hair gone up in smoke and you ask me how much it's worth.'

POHLMANN: Some things are beyond money.

MISS WEBER: Really? I've yet to find them.

POHLMANN: We'd all rather have our health than the money.

MISS WEBER: Correction. We'd all rather have our health *and* the money.

KAFKA: You are asking for a justice that doesn't exist in the world. And not only you. More people. More people every year.

(KAFKA *is looking through the files on the table and finds one.*) A man works in the carding room of a cotton mill. Dust everywhere. The air dust. Taken ill. Examined by the company doctor. Unfit for work. Discharged. Nothing unusual in that. Except somebody decides to put in a P48, a claim for compensation, just as you did.

MISS WEBER: Not applicable. Either of them. Not accidents.

KAFKA: Quite. But bear with me. Take this millworker. No beam has fallen on his head. No bottle has exploded in his eye. He has not got his shirt caught in the shaft and been taken round. All that has happened is that he has been inhaling cotton dust for some years. And day by day this cotton dust has crept into his lungs, but so slowly, so gradually that it cannot be called an accident. But suppose our lungs were not internal organs. Suppose they were not locked away in the chest. Suppose we carried our lungs outside our bodies, bore them before us, could hold and handle them, cradle them in our arms. And suppose further they were not made of flesh but of glass, or something like glass, not yet invented, something pliable. And thus the effect of each breath could be seen, the deposit of each intake of air, calculated, weighed even. What would we say then, as we saw the dust accumulate, the passages clog, the galleries close down, as cell by cell these lungs hardened, withered, died. Mm?

POHLMANN: But that still wouldn't be an accident. You can't conduct an insurance company on suppositions like that, can you?

KAFKA: And if we were able to magnify each inhalation, see under the microscope each breath, capture the breath that killed the cell, register the gasp that caused the cough that broke the vein that atrophied the flesh. Wouldn't that be an accident? A very small accident? This man has no claim because he is suffering from a condition. But isn't a condition the result of many small accidents that we cannot see or record?

POHLMANN: But so is living. Or dying. There is no alternative but to breathe.

KAFKA: And this man. A young man. So regularly doused in dye he has begun to grow a second skin. Isn't that an accident? A long slow accident?

MISS WEBER: People will be wanting compensation for being
  alive next.
  (KAFKA *looks as if this might not be a bad idea.*)
KAFKA: I do understand.
FRANZ: What good is that to me? You can't do anything. You're
  worse than them, not better. You say you understand; well,
  if you understand and you don't help, you're wicked, you're
  evil.
MISS WEBER: Don't speak like that to Doctor Kafka. He has a
  university degree.
  (KAFKA *begins to take out his wallet.*)
FRANZ: I don't want money.
  (FRANZ *rises.* KAFKA *follows him.*)
KAFKA: I am not offering you money.
  (*They leave the office.* KAFKA *gives* FRANZ *a card.*)
  I know of a factory that is starting. It will be in a month or
  two.
  (*They move off down the corridor which runs between the
  offices.*)
FRANZ: This is a terrible place.
KAFKA: Is it? I always forget that. I find it . . . almost cosy. But
  then I'm just an official. I am accustomed to office air.
  (*They stop at the end of the corridor.*)
  If you cannot find a job I may be able to help.
  (KAFKA *shakes hands. When* FRANZ *has gone* KAFKA *removes
  some small bits of skin that have adhered to his hand.*)

INT. AN EMPTY FACTORY. DAY
*The high ornate door of an empty factory, with a huge rose window.
Inside the factory there is a rope hanging down attached to a sack. We
hear* KAFKA's *brother-in-law before he enters.*
BROTHER-IN-LAW: (*Out of vision*) Don't expect anything too
  wonderful. It's very rudimentary. Well, one factory is very
  much like another.
  (KAFKA *enters the factory with his* BROTHER-IN-LAW.)
  But why am I telling you? You've got expertise. You know
  about factories. You've seen plenty. (*Pause.*) It's not as if I'm
  asking you to go into something blindfold.

(*They are now up on a higher floor.*)
And here; shipments could come in and out. You see, you
see. It's ideal. I know I can succeed, Franz. Do you ever
have that feeling?

KAFKA: Only when I'm very depressed.

(*They walk down steps and out of shot. Mix through to:*)

INT. CHRISTINA'S PARENTS' APARTMENT. NIGHT
FRANZ *sits awkwardly in the formal room with his fiancée*
CHRISTINA, *and the* OLD LADY *in the wheelchair.* CHRISTINA
reaches out to him. FRANZ *says nothing, then stands up and to*
CHRISTINA'S *horror starts to remove his clothes. The* OLD LADY
watches. The GIRL *is horrified by the disfigurement of his skin. She*
runs out of the room.

CHRISTINA: Mother! Father!

(FRANZ *stands there, naked, looking at the* OLD LADY, *who*
looks at him without emotion. Christina's MOTHER *looks in,*
shrieks and closes the door. Christina's FATHER *opens the door,*
stares wordlessly, and closes the door. Then CHRISTINA *very*
nervously opens the door, and gets hold of the wheelchair and
takes the OLD LADY *out. Her* SISTER *closes the door. There is*
silence. FRANZ *sits down. He seems quite tranquil. There are*
whisperings and muttered conversations outside the door. Finally
the door opens and CHRISTINA *comes in and throws something*
on to the sofa, next to where FRANZ *is sitting.* FRANZ *picks it*
up. It is the engagement ring. Mix through to:)

INT. NEW FACTORY. DAY
KAFKA *at the new factory. A busy atmosphere and noticeably dusty.*
KAFKA *coughing, handkerchief over his mouth, as he supervises the*
work. His BROTHER-IN-LAW *comes up to him with a message.*

BROTHER-IN-LAW: Franz, Franz, some people to see you in the
office.

(*We track* FRANZ *and* BROTHER-IN-LAW *through to:*)

INT. FACTORY OFFICE. DAY
BROTHER-IN-LAW: (*As they enter the office*) Coughing still?

KAFKA: No.

BROTHER-IN-LAW: (*Jubilantly*) This is something to cough about. Three more orders this morning. I'm run off my feet. (*He exits up the stairs.* FRANZ *is waiting in the office.* KAFKA *smiles and shakes hands.*)

KAFKA: So you're still interested in the job?

FRANZ: Yes. Very much so.

KAFKA: You look well.

FRANZ: Yes, I'm better. My skin cleared completely. (*Shows him his hands.*) A miracle.

KAFKA: Why is that, do you think?

FRANZ: I don't know. I've never been so well.

(*A* GIRL *is sitting in the background.*)

This is my fiancée, Beatrice.

(*The* GIRL *moves towards them and we see it is not Christina, but the girl from the dyeworks office, who, at the start of the film, told him to ask about insurance.*)

KAFKA: Let me show you.

(*The three of them go through into the factory.*)

FRANZ: So what is it you're producing here?

KAFKA: Building materials. Mainly asbestos.

(FRANZ *shakes hands with* KAFKA.)

FRANZ: Thank you. You saved my life.

(*Mix through to:*)

INT. DOCTOR'S CONSULTING ROOM, PRAGUE. NIGHT. 1945

FRANZ (OLD) *and the* DOCTOR *are standing by the X-ray.*

FRANZ: It's so long ago. But you think it may have been that factory?

DOCTOR: It's possible. Who knows?

(*They walk through to the consulting room.*)

FRANZ: (*On their way out*) I was happy working there, though it was only for a year or two. The place went bankrupt. They say no good deed goes unpunished. He worked there too, Doctor Kafka, part-time, so I suppose the same thing could have happened to him.

(*They stop by the door.*)

DOCTOR: You weren't to know. He wasn't to know. You
     breathed, that's all you did wrong.
     (*Pause. They move off down the stairs.*)
     You breathed in the wrong place.
FRANZ: I've a feeling he died. But he was a Jew, so he would
     have died anyway.
DOCTOR: Mmm. I know the name. They sold fancy goods. I
     bought some slippers there once.
     (*He and* FRANZ *are now at the outside door. He opens it and we
     see on the road the shadow of a corpse hanging from a lamp-
     post.*)
     I wonder how long they're going to leave that body up there.
     (*Shakes his head.*) I heard him battering at some door last
     night, begging to be let in. Somebody was after him. Then
     the door was opened and he thought he was safe. But they
     were there first. Take care.
     (*They shake hands.* FRANZ *goes out into the street and the*
     DOCTOR *closes the door. Then exits up the stairs. Hold on the
     closed door for the credits, seeing the corpse shadow through the
     glass.*)